BETRAYAL

A PERSONAL STORY

"I need your help," he said,
and that was only the start.

BETRAYAL

A PERSONAL STORY

"I need your help," he said,
and that was only the start.

JS AYLIFFE

PEPPER PRESS

First published in 2026 by Pepper Press, an imprint of Fair Play Publishing

PO Box 4101, Balgowlah Heights, NSW 2093, Australia

www.fairplaypublishing.com.au

ISBN: 978-1-923236-42-4

ISBN: 978-1-923236-43-1 (ePub)

Design and typesetting by Leslie Priestley

Front cover illustration by Cathy Wilcox

All inquiries should be made to the Publisher via hello@fairplaypublishing.com.au

A catalogue record of this book is available from the National Library of Australia.

In Memory of
IAN LAWTHER
(1958-2024)

*"...and I think about Jesus, how much he loved children,
how he said that children were of the kingdom of God."*
**JON FOSSE
2023 NOBEL PRIZE
FOR LITERATURE**

*"The present crisis in the Church must be compared
with the Reformation and French Revolution."*
**BISHOP JOHN QUINN,
1929-2017**

*"The dying Jews are surrounded only by Pontius Pilates who wash their hands
of the issue. This silence cannot be tolerated any longer. Whatever the grounds
may be, it is disgraceful. Whoever remains silent when faced with murder
becomes the murderer's accomplice. Anyone who does not condemn, consents.
It is the requirement of our Christian conscience. We do not want to be Pilates."*
ZOFIA KOSSAK-SRCZUCKA: "Protest"
Oskar Schindler Museum, Krakow, Poland

*"Every three minutes /a woman is beaten/every five minutes /a woman is raped/
every ten minutes/a lil girl is molested/yet I rode the subway today."*
NTOZAKE SHANGE, poet, 1948-2018

"But what about the children?" asked Ivan.
"How will we ever account for their sufferings?"
FYODOR DOSTOEVSKY,
The Brothers Karamasov

"From today's crisis, will emerge a Church that has lost a great deal.
It will become small and will have to start pretty much all over again."
JOSEPH RATZINGER,
priest, prophesying on German radio in 1967

"The Church needs to go broke to be revitalised."
FATHER KEVIN DILLON,
Lifeboat Geelong Foundation

"Jesus used to be a kid, too."
America Magazine,
February 2024

'I need your help,' he said, and that was only the start.

Contents

Author's Note

In 1990, when I worked in advertising, I found myself complicit in a crime when I was asked to help cover-up the sexual abuse against children committed by members of the Marist Brothers Order of the Catholic Church. As there were no witnesses to that discussion, it was a case of 'his word against mine'.

Consequently, I was forced to live with the moment, and it wasn't until the revelations of the *Royal Commission into Institutional Responses to Child Sexual Abuse* and the instigator of that cover-up was outed that, set free of my shame, I knew I had to write this book. I believe, as Nelson Mandela said, reconciliation arrives through truth.

The soul of Catholicism is wounded and needs a new shepherd of the people, one who would rescue the Church from its betrayers and traitors and reset it on the path set by *Jesus of Nazareth, a Person Like Us,* as the Jesuit, Roger Lenaers, says in his 1948 book of that title.

The 4th century had seen an early father of the Catholic Church, St Irenaeus, Bishop of Lyon, declare the Church's 'home is where the people are'. It was an idea reprised by a more recent Church saint, the beloved Pope John XXIII, who in 1959 told all those gathered at the Second Vatican Council: 'You are the Church.'

I urge you to get hold of Austin Ivereigh's biography of the world's greatest leader of recent times: *The Wounded Shepherd: Pope Francis and his Struggle to Convert the Catholic Church.*

'We must think of the little ones,' said this remarkable Argentinian upon his inauguration in 2013. Was this his Nelson Mandela moment, that promises redemption in truth-telling and justice for the thousands hurt by institutional indifference to the crimes that have torn the Catholic Church apart?

We can only hope!

J S AYLIFFE

Prologue

The night is still; through a window a feast of lights – streetlights and house lights, – and in the distance the Manly Wharf is bathed in yellow. Shadows of its pylons wash the steely water; an occasional ferry, long and impressive, slides through the darkness taking the last of the tourists and partygoers back to the city.

This is my home.

Dominant in the background and high on a hill, the mustard sandstone edifice people around here still call the "Bishop's castle" is fully lit up in soft, gold light.

There is no man of the cloth in residence now, and the seminarians are long gone.

Today, in a sign of the times, the building is leased from the Catholic Church by the International School of Hospitality. Food for the stomach, perhaps not the soul.

Another of Catholicism's prized icons has bitten the dust.

Once resided there a man who, it has been said, had designs on becoming Pope.

One
MEA CULPA

2014
Downfall

'In 1989 – the year we are talking about – you were Provincial of the Catholic Order of Marists?'

'That is correct.'

His turn in the box, he shifts uneasily and is reminded he had once overseen over two thousand celibate men of Christ, and here he is being asked to answer for the misdemeanors of a few.

How could he have known? People have secrets and that was more so then; things were hushed up but the faithful believed they could trust their children's educators and he was always saddened when parents had been let down. Now, 25 years later, he is being forced to answer questions; the chickens have come home to roost, and he is in the firing line.

Words formed invisibly on his lips, and he begins to pray silently – 'Hail Mary full of grace...'

He breaks off; under such serious scrutiny he is unable to continue with the most sacred prayer of the Marists; it doesn't seem right. Heaven may forbid it, but at that moment, he was lost to the mother of God.

Isn't the rosary what holds us together during the dark times of our souls? Central to what makes the Marist Order different – the love and adoration of Mary – it was only recently he had found a special religious text that described that difference. There is a word: *charism,* "the power given by the Holy Spirit", and now it seems everything is about to be shattered – everything and – he believes – *through no fault of his own*. Now he is being forced to defend his beloved centuries-old Order of Marist Brothers; he is already afraid that no matter what he has to say, the actions of his errant Brothers were *in*defensible.

He straightens visibly and adjusts his glasses.

He is a small man with intense blue eyes and Celtic skin that has never been able to endure too much sun. Now in his 65th year and balding, he has always enjoyed sports, coached rugby and, playing tennis in the sunburnt country, these days he keeps covered up and out of the elements whenever he can.

The Marist leader has been a man of stature among the Brothers; professorially certain of his words; used to occupying high positions in the Catholic Church he is prepared to protect the faith at all costs. The world is a dangerous place and ever since Luther Catholicism, it has been under threat.

Earlier, he had resolved to throw off any attempt at guardedness; being on the defensive has its habit of implying guilt; yes, he would answer their questions; but he had prepared himself to meet the secularists and their law head on.

After 25 years, the day he had been dreading has come; he is on his own. And the Commission wants the truth.

The *world* has been waiting; I am waiting. For far too long, our demons have been dancing with both of us; and now is the hour we will both dance with them.

<><>

1990
Two Voices, Betrayal

This morning, I had a phone call from a friend: he leads a teaching Brotherhood in the Catholic Church. He needs my help, urgently. Surprised by the suddenness of his request, I accepted nonetheless, and we settled on today, 2 o'clock. I cancelled my usual Friday lunchtime run with business friends and have headed out west to his current home on the outer reaches of Sydney Harbour. It is late winter; spring has come early; the plovers are sitting on their eggs in the wide-open spaces of grassy parks and golf courses; were it not for the poison barbs on the wings of the males, they would be stupid birds. Every living thing needs protection.

The Marist leader oversees a vast community of celibate men. The Marist Order insists on a vow of poverty, the Provincial House in Sydney is like many Catholic presbyteries I have come to know. For one thing it is solid, but it is also sombre – they always are – made of dark brick and stone with deep sash windows, some that work, others that probably haven't in years. Imposing on a large block of land right beside the Parramatta River, a lay person with the necessaries would have soon brought such a cold and unprepossessing home into the modern world, and with all its pre-requisite comforts. But the building and land were probably a gift from a wealthy Catholic, unrenovated; spend money wisely, use it for the less fortunate.

I am just 14 years a Catholic and confess to still being starry-eyed by the original Christian faith. It had been sensibly humanised by the great and saintly Pope John XXIII after he brought all the "red hats" together in his hastily convened Second Vatican Council: his mission was to save the Church from its tired self. My belief is grounded in Jesuit rationality and in Christ's singular commandment to "love one another". Always wanting to help, I have had no hesitation in responding to my friend's call.

The man I know is serious-minded, some would say humourless; a scientist by training, he has been a headmaster and rugby coach in his time. A straightforward man, I know he is not one to argue with. But he is well-read in Church doctrine and spirituality and has been bringing his reading of it to the discussion group my wife and I began some time ago. We have come to know him as a friend.

He is usually calm and always appears to be on top of his game, hence I was surprised by the tenor of his phone call. Along with the sense of urgency conveyed, he had said he was 'hoping you could make it this afternoon'. Something was up.

I undo the latch on the wrought-iron gate. The heavy metal is cold to my touch, and I blow on my hands before rubbing them together to warm them. My breath mists visibly in the July weather, and I head along the concrete path that separates lawns cut low. A short post with a telltale net mechanism is the only surviving remnant of the tennis court that once stood there. Rose bushes, recently pruned, cling to the perimeter; they aren't out now, but must be quite a spectacle when they are. This is where he lives, lucky him; although the lonely life he has chosen would be too high a price for me to pay, with no hope of a family and forced to live without sex – supposedly. Isn't celibacy an archaic Catholic rule that had been created to avoid the complications of inheritance? Personally, I think it is a crazy rule, one that is wide open to hypocrisy.

<>

I have reached the house and mount the old, cracked stone steps and cross the faded tiled veranda to the entrance.

The doorway is large and stately, but it is more. One could walk a horse through it, and somebody probably once did. There's a sturdy wrought-iron security door, locked, behind which a massive timber door is half open. Its stained-glass inset catches the late-morning sun, but it is only half-inviting, being dark within.

Out of the gloom emerges his familiar face. He is rattling a bunch of keys. Selecting one, the largest, he drives it into the ancient lock, and I step back as the heavy iron door is pushed outwards. Why all the security? The paranoia?

'Thanks for coming.' I am ushered inside, with some urgency.

The Marist leader is routinely dressed in faded brown trousers, a lightly checked shirt, open neck; ordinariness all the go since Vatican II brought the

Church's clerics closer to the people. Many are incognito now, like spies. They can get away with all sorts and probably do. I note his face has a sickly pallor; his eyes are small and sunken, fixed; they rarely meet another's, and today they are bloodshot, as though tired of responsibility and maybe of life.

'I came when I could.'

'Fine,' he says, and he proffers an outstretched hand. His demeanour is leaden, and I accept the gesture as nothing more than a formality. He turns toward a long, gloomy hallway and urges me to follow in haste. Something is up.

He has been nervous from the start. He hurries us on.

Soon, we are in an enormous, cold kitchen, one that obviously serves as the Brothers' dining room. Obedient to the style of this place, there is a large, ironwood refectory table that appears small by the size of the room; high-back wooden chairs stand six to a side, a single carver, throne-like, at one end; his seat, perhaps?

I am urged to join him on one of the side chairs – he will be no high and mighty Church leader today, as I have found those in Catholicism's high echelons can be – and we sit together in an intimate, equal arrangement. A housekeeper arrives instantly with tea, biscuits and the ubiquitous – common to all religious gatherings in my experience – cake. The housekeeper is also standard, being on the overweight side, aproned, wears no make-up, smiles chubbily, and doesn't speak more than is necessary to do her job.

The housekeeper is diligent and pours the tea so slowly her employer grows impatient. Out of character for him, he begins tapping his fingers on the table. He is nervous. Already balding, he appears to have lost more of his grey hair. He has seen less sun lately; his skin is so pale it would fry on a sunbeam. Right now, his rimless glasses are slightly slanted. My friend is a troubled man who hasn't slept. Perhaps it is why I haven't seen much of him lately.

The housekeeper finishes with the pouring and leaves us obediently; they must have spoken. I hear her heavy feet on the stairs. She will be well out of earshot and sight. Alone now with me, he is agitated, his voice hoarse.

'I need your help desperately. Our centuries-old Order is under threat,' he says forthrightly, although he gives nothing away.

What to say? I have been there before when this comprehensively serious man appeared to be even more so. At this moment, he has fallen seriously silent; his evasive eyes have dimmed. I have given a nod to show that I want to know more and understand what is going on.

But the conversation does not move on, and the pause reminds me our group recently made a foray into psychology. It was his suggestion that we explore the Myers-Briggs Typology Indicator, whereupon he was defined as *ISTJ*, which, according to the test, means he is an Introvert, Sensing, Thinker and Judger, the exact opposite of me (Extrovert, Intuitive, Feeler and Perceiver, or *ENFP*). In one sense, his type doesn't beat about the bush but thinks before speaking, while my tendency is to talk to think. Right now, he is out of character. He appears lost. It is up to me to begin the conversation.

I ask: 'How can I help?'

He doesn't answer the question, saying instead: 'Our very future may depend upon what you and your people can do for us.'

'I see. (*I don't: he wants us to help him raise money?* says the voice in my head.)

He places a hand on the table and turns to me. 'I have a PR problem and require immediate action,' he says, with surprising knowledge of the way things work with the media.

'Oh,' I reply, acknowledging his need but requiring more information.

He fidgets furtively, offering me another cup of tea that he pours with a shaky hand. (*What problem? For God's sake, get on with it.*)

He waves a languid hand in the air in a sad and gloomy manner, and with an evasive gesture stands and walks away a few steps (maybe it has all been a mistake and the meeting will be over before it has begun); then he turns, presenting me with an uncommonly sad stare.

'One of my men has been doing things he shouldn't.'

'With what, money?' (*He has given me no inkling, why be so evasive, expect me to guess?*)

He falls into the chair beside me with a thud. 'With little boys.'

(*No! I hope the Brother he speaks of isn't teaching any of our children, Helen's and mine; maybe – it doesn't bear to think – that's why our eldest ran away from the esteemed college we are sending our boys to, all four soon to have a taste of boarding school.*)

It is all I can do to hold back my anger. I am staring in disbelief and disgust at my – my friend.

'You know you are talking about a serious crime?'

'It could be the ruin of us,' he replies, waving the truth away.

(*That all you can say?*) I contain myself: 'Not if you do the right thing.'

(*The truth will set you free.*)

I search his face and find his eyes have strangely hardened. 'That's why I need you,' he says before pausing. 'Especially you. I require your expertise.'

(I am confused): 'Have you been to the police?'

(*After all, it's a crime, blood on the hands*). He shakes his head violently, it seems the law is the last thing he needs.

'I need your PR skills.'

(Now it is my turn to pause and get my head around this – this terrible, shameful turn of events – but the voice in my head is telling me I am not hearing much compassion here, it is as if, to him, he is facing not much more than an inadvertent mistake: after all, *child rape* is "kiddy-fiddling" to some.)

He is waiting impatiently for my answer, and I am telling myself there is only one thing I can say; but perhaps it won't be what he wishes to hear.

Finally: 'I see. I fully understand. But you need help when you talk to the police. That is not PR, that is a lawyer. You need a solicitor. I can help you with that. You must go to the police,' I insist.

He stands and takes a few steps away, then turns. 'But – you don't understand.'

'You think?' (*No, I do understand; I understand perfectly well. In religion it is so often survival before empathy, no matter the truth; and right now for me, accepting that is hard. I feel the sadness of knowing deep inside:* 'These are children, we are talking about children,' I want to say, in what will become the premise of this book.

But I don't.

Not yet.

Is it worth having one last crack at his better nature? He is – I smart at the realisation – one of the smartest people I know. What's to convince?

'You are talking about a crime,' I say.

I lock his eyes onto mine and tell him he doesn't have any other option.

After a while, the police idea is quickly dismissed. 'I can't. These are my Brothers,' he says forlornly, and as if there may be more felons among his flock.

He says he called me because he is convinced I have the answer. 'You have told me you have been doing work for the government.'

'Yes. In child protection.'

'*Protection,*' I repeat. 'I'm on the other side of the fence.' With the defenders and protectors.

I have fallen into disbelief; I don't believe what I am hearing. My inner voice is moving from confusion to downright anger and despair. But he is visibly desperate and turns away from my uncomprehending eyes. He will confess, he is at the end of his tether.

'I didn't know who else to turn to. You once told me,' he says faltering before clearing his throat – 'you have said with the work you have been engaged in, you have learnt there are some – such people – who say they can't help it.'

(*But what's to understand about that? Those – "such people" are abusing kids! cries my inner voice as I contemplate what I am seeing to be his now complete lack of empathy for the victims of one of the worst crimes imaginable*).

'This is really bad,' I remind him (speaking to his desperate attempt to protect his men), 'and nobody will offer you sympathy. Nobody. You must inform the police.' I pause for a moment. 'Which school are you talking about? Or is it schools?'

(*Remembering the Marist leader helped get my boys into St Joseph's College, I am horrified by the thought my children might be in danger; and it is suddenly showing*).

He ignores the question, gazing at me intently.

'Can I expect you to help us, or not?' he asked with pronounced frustration.

(*My stomach begins to churn. It is difficult enough, this conversation I have been drawn into with someone I thought I knew as a friend. But he doesn't know what he is getting into.*)

'You have to go to the police,' I repeat, appealing to his better judgement. I tell him firmly and for the umpteenth time that he has no choice.

I remind him we have been talking about the worst of crimes – child molestation.

'Victims never get over it. The abused self-harm. They grow to be addicts and alcoholics. They suicide.'

I steel myself and tell him many people say that there's only one thing to do with child rapists: they should throw away the key.

When he smarts at that, I remind him – I know it will be the last time I say it – that I can help find him the right channels. 'I can get you someone who will hold your hand when you talk to the police. You'll need a lawyer with experience in crimes against children, and I can help you with that.'

'*Crimes?*' he exclaims with considerable affront. 'Is that what you call them?'

Of course, "them". So, it is a serial issue. I return his gaze intently and appeal to the better angels of a man I thought I knew. 'We are talking about molesting

- *raping!* –children. We are talking about the murder of the soul,' I say, hoping the religious context will open his heart.

He appears to acknowledge what I have said.

But he remains unmoved.

He is suddenly almost violent when he declares: 'I won't allow my Brothers – or the Church – to be destroyed. Our enemies have been out to destroy the Catholic Church ever since the Reformation.' (I am reminded that the history of the Church has always been controlled by the Vatican.)

'Even before that,' he says, conjuring visions of the Roman colonists putting a price on the head of the new Christians that they saw as a threat, sending assassins out to kill them. But this is side-tracking, and he knows it.

'Rape is forever,' I say, hoping my sudden familiarity will change things. 'The kids never forget. Nobody forgets being raped.'

But he doesn't want to hear. 'They're gunning for us,' he repeats with certain finality.

'They will be.' Now it is my time to be overly forceful. 'As sure as Hell, if you don't hand over the criminals you may be hiding. The law is the law.'

When he shifts about irritably and his eyes are vacant, I know I have touched a nerve of the present supreme hierarch of the Marist Brothers across the Southern Hemisphere. 'The Church is the Church,' he replies.

The sacred Catholic Church! It always comes first, in all things. No matter the circumstances, the almighty Catholic Church sees itself as bigger than the law of the land.

He fidgets with the Marist badge that never leaves the lapel of his cassock (*I remember he gave me a set of cufflinks once, the ecclesiastic M, gold with a halo on deep blue – what to do with them now?*), and at first there is another stony silence.

Then, 'I hope you understand what I am being forced to do,' he says. 'I appeal to you as a friend of the Order. You must see the predicament I am in. There are over two thousand Marist Brothers across Australia and the Pacific Islands, they are my people, and I am responsible for all of them.'

(*So?*)

I glance at the cross that is high on the wall and wish Christ would come down from it and finish the job he started. My new-found adversary briefly follows my gaze, before turning to me helplessly and I know there will be no resurrection – no redemption – today.

Instead, he quotes more statistics: 'The Marists have been around for over two hundred years.'

He gestures towards the heavy security door. We are done.

Except we are not, and I know, as a man of power, he will want the final word. But I have never been so unprepared, as I will be when he is soon nervously fumbling with the large, archaic key, and suddenly pauses, gazing at me curiously through the wrought iron, and says: 'You know, some boys can be provocative.'

(*No! You don't believe that! Not the man of God I once knew. You don't believe what you are saying – although maybe you do.*)

I am hanging onto my own faith, Christ's cross, by my fingernails. I will fight fire with fire with words I have wanted to give voice to ever since I had arrived at Marist headquarters to hear the worst. I will give voice to my first thought.

'We hand over our kids to be educated, *not fucked over* by your men. We're not talking about *kiddy-fiddling* here, as you insist the raping of a child is,' I tell him, calmly, truthfully, hoping to find his better angel. 'You have made me party to your cover-up, and I don't like it. Please, please, go to the police, for the sake of both our skins,' I say, knowing that, under the circumstances, it is up to him. 'We could both go to jail. Along with your *paedophile* Brothers. I assume there are lots more of them.'

But all I am greeted with is a cold, hard stare that has come up from the depths of his very being.

He has already turned away and disappeared into the darkness; he hasn't heard me. He has decisions to make, but it seems the law of the land is of no matter to a man of the cloth who believes the metaphorical "they" are always out to get the Church.

Forget the horrors of its clerics' crimes.

The "enemies" of the Catholic Church are, in the Marist leader's eyes, everywhere.

I am in a classic entrapment: for as long as it takes to bring about justice, what has taken place between the Marist leader and me will always be his word against mine; he will make sure of that.

('They're out to get us.')

<>

And now I am struggling to get away from this place, and its terrible secrets. I am sick to my stomach and unsure even where I parked the car.

I am walking up the path: the rose bushes on either side of me are nothing but sticks now; wait for the spring to see them in full bloom; their vibrant colours, their sweet perfumes. Afficionados will rejoice, the bees will be buzzing about, their melodious anthem heralding warm nights and joyous days at the beach.

But I can't see that now and am remembering a poem by Spike Milligan, that has speared into my heart; its author never scared of the truth.

> "The new rose
> trembles with early beauty
> The babe sees the beckoning carmine,
> the tiny hand
> clutches the cruel stem.
> The babe screams,
> The rose is silent –
> Life is already telling lies."
> *Small Dreams of a Scorpion, 1972*

<>

Truth is supposed to set us free, but, caged as I am by it, there is the intimate reality, that there is not much worse than to be gypped by a friend, especially a man of the cloth I thought I knew.

With dark thoughts for company, the streets appear empty, though they're not. I inadvertently kick a dog, out with its master, who, strangely is the one to apologise as the dog whimpers. I nod – "sorry" – as they continue on their way, and I resume mine.

Driven ever deeper into a well of loneliness, I struggle with the thought that more children may be in danger – my children – at the hands of the Catholic Church.

In 1990, St Joseph's College is an elite Marist boarding school and famed rugby nursery of some 700 boys; and although numbers have been declining within the Order and the ratio of Brothers to lay teachers is widening by the year, there's still a bunch of celibate men all living in, many as dorm-masters. Conservative Catholics would like to think the sexual revolution has passed them by, but now it seems such hope is an aberration; although, much to the detriment of the many wonderful, knowledgeable teachers among the teaching Orders, it only takes one. Paedophiles are hard to detect for they are protected by their secrecy.

I am weakened and by the time I reach the car, my stomach is turning and will continue to do so as, fighting anxiety, I drive in a daze on autopilot back to the office.

I park haphazardly, stumbling up the stairs.

Sally, my long-time secretary, asks me how the meeting with the Churchman went, and I reply weakly, 'it was ok.' But we have been there before – she knows when a meeting has gone badly.

'I'll get you a cup of tea,' she says, expecting me to tell her I'm going to the pub with anyone who will join me, but that would mean being put on the spot and having the truth about what happened dragged out of me. 'It was a storm in a teacup, and I couldn't help,' I say to Sally, catching her in mid-stride before she closes the door.

'Well, that's alright then,' she says, and we know neither of us has been entirely truthful.

Sally and I have been working together for some ten years and when she returns with the tea, I know she has read my state of mind. She is a brown-eyed blonde and with her big, open heart, she continually falls for the wrong man. Like any good secretary, she knows me backwards and has got me out of many a scrape when I forget where I am supposed to be. But this time I must not confide in her. I am left with my despairing thoughts and questions I know will not have the right answers:

Should I call the police? Oh, how I want to. And if so, what is there to say? I can hear the law: *'So, you say there were just the two of you? It is your word against his?'* I would find myself taking on the Catholic Church; with its vast wealth, I'd be doomed.

Soon, I am sipping the fourth or fifth cup of tea of the day, tossing up whether now is the time for something stronger, when I cannot bear the anxiety one more minute and head out once again, this time intending to go straight home.

<>

Why did I choose these cliff tops to contemplate what has happened? Do I want to jump? A young, disturbed man recently did, to his death; nobody saw him, nobody knew; but everybody knew he was a basket case, and when he failed to turn up for work, somebody knew where he went in his dark times –

because his body was quickly found.

And what of me? I'm here, now, steeling myself to tell my wife. There are no secrets between us and secrets shared lessen the pain. Don't they?

We will face the music together for as long as it takes, hoping the friend we once knew will soon come to his senses and – well, think of the children who will suffer the hurt forever that was inflicted upon them by one of the Brothers, and on his watch. Perhaps he might care to think of *our* kids?

But – 'Some young boys can be provocative,' he had said – and he believed it, which is more the outrage.

<>

No! I can't believe he said it.

Some boys are lonely. They're missing home (and easy bait for a *paedophile*. Especially when it's late at night, the boys' dormitory is quiet, and everyone but two of its occupants are asleep).

Spike Milligan's scorpion poem is screaming in my head.

Soon, I am stuck in a nightmare of my own.

<><>

1990
The Grooming

'Come in,' the dorm Brother announces languidly in response to the gentle tapping that has been interrupting his sleep. By the time the boy enters his room, the dorm Brother has dragged himself out of bed and roughly thrown a blanket around his shoulders; copious, it touches the floor.

The Brother couldn't believe his luck when joining the Order to be close to children, he was put in charge of a dormitory in the large, elite boarding school. Forty-seven of the little devils, and all with "potential". Has his most fervent wish been granted?

'What's the matter, boy, you should be asleep?' he enquires of the small, teary country lad.

'I don't know, I can't stop crying, Bro. What's the matter with me, Bro?'

Bro – it took him a while to get used to the affectionate way the boys address their superiors. 'Come here, you dear, sweet boy,' says the dorm Brother, and quickly has him inside. 'Shut the door lad, we don't want to wake the others, do we?'

The dorm Brother's bedroom is also his study. Books line the walls; there is a desk and large chair. He sits on the chair and beckons the lonely boy to sit on his knee. The boy wipes his eyes with an elbow and obliges.

'You are homesick, that's all,' says the dorm Brother, and pats the head that has nestled into his neck. He reaches the blanket across them both.

'Everybody misses their home,' he whispers. 'It's natural – like lots of things that we don't understand,' he says, and kisses the lad on his crown.

'I can't sleep,' he hears the boy say and lifts him onto the floor, whereupon the boy turns, gazes up at the Bro with lazy, wet eyes, and pleads with him to be allowed to stay a bit longer.

'Only for a little while,' says the dorm Brother comfortingly. 'Now we both need sleep. I am sure you are allowed to get into your parents' bed on occasion.'

'Yes, I do,' says the boy quietly.

The boy finds an arm around his shoulders and he is held tight.

The dorm Brother sings softly:

"Silent night, holy night,
All is calm, all is bright..."

The boy will be back in his own bed long before dawn, not knowing he has been groomed.

Meanwhile, the dorm Brother will have been in a reverie of some time anticipation the entire time. He has long been aware of his affliction.

He is the "man who loves children", *Lolita's* Humbert Humbert, a fictional creation that most inspired him:

"Light of my life, fire of my loins…my sin, my soul…standing four feet ten in one sock…there might have been no *Lolita* at all had I not loved, one summer, a certain initial girl-child."

Nabokov's Humbert Humbert had preyed on a young girl, but hadn't the dorm Brother joined the Marists, partly to claim his own boy-child?

Recently it was put to him that a suspicious mother had gone to the headmaster about – what she apparently said – is his liking to enfold young children in his robes. Fortunately for him, that didn't go far; neither did another mum's questioning why he asked his Year 7 dormitory to bring their teddy bears with them to school. Didn't he think 'teenage boys would have left their dolls behind by now?'

'Yes, that does seem strange,' said the head, apparently, and that, as far as the school was concerned, was that.

He, the dorm Brother, had retained his position, after a narrow escape; but opportunity remained.

The next little while will see him forced to be extra vigilant. But such is a life so dependent upon secrecy, guile and cunning.

<><>

1990
The Cover-ups Expand

The talk of bullying did seem harmless at the time, and the parents' meeting would have dismissed it were it not that the boy, who had supposedly been the object, had been suddenly taken out of school.

'He disappeared overnight,' said our youngest son, genuinely surprised.

I had to admit the decision seemed rash. It would have been extra tough, what with the boy's father being an old boy of the school (Joey's old boys are a special breed, joined to the elite college at the hip).

Of course, the meeting thought the bullying story had instant veracity, coming as it did from the headmaster himself. No one was about to question the man at the top, and that left me cringingly uneasy: were we all about to be involved in another cover-up?

(Later, I will learn that the boy's parents had informed others of the truth, and the real reason why they had taken their child elsewhere, only to be lambasted for criticising 'such a fine school'.)

Things seemed to be getting out of hand, the cover-ups would eventually be far-reaching. But I am comforted knowing most boys usually stick together; mine have made good, loyal friends.

Friends protect one another.

As for the college, I once asked the headmaster, who I see to be a fair-minded disciplinarian, how he controlled so much high testosterone 'when my wife and I are flat out with four boys of our own?'

I hope he remembers what he said: 'We keep them busy and remind them they are there for one another.'

"Strength and honesty in adversity" is the school motto and it has a hard-fought image to live up to, of sporting – and hopefully academic – glory, and 150 years of turning out well-rounded young men.

And yet, while the molestation of an angelic kid who is missing his mother has pierced the thin veneer of its respectability, will the school's fragile power structure hold? Or will it go on to hide terrible secrets and blatant lies? I don't expect to have the answer anytime soon.

'They're gunning for us,' he had said, and I fear those words will guide the Marists – and the Church – until the fragile house of cards comes tumbling down.

And, as my shame takes hold, little do I do know that for 24 years my subsequent state of mind will bring about bewildering and occasional outbursts that will arrive seemingly out of nowhere. I will be irrational during those episodic times when, like Spike, whose mother was always there for him, it will be my wife's moral strength that will be the final arbiter of things between us, our marriage, our minds and spirit – her innate ability to save me from myself, even in the darkest moments, when I think I am going crazy and don't know why.

Such – I will learn – is the power of deep-seated anxiety, the breaking out of truths put away, but not ever put to bed.

Meanwhile, my well-being will come to depend upon extreme exercise, surfing in the dawn light and the marathons that produce those friendly endorphins during the time on the road.

In 1977 I had chosen to become a Catholic; I had completed the trinity of persons learnt at a Protestant boarding school, that we are "body, mind and spirit", and I remain a believer, though hanging on by the skin of my teeth. Now that decision will be tested like it never has been before.

I pray: 'Holy Mary, mother of God, pray for us sinners, now and at the hour of our death, Amen.'

I pray the prayer given to me by a Jesuit, who had once mentored me: 'Heal me, strengthen my Faith and share your Peace with me.'

These days, I search for the Christ that's within us, and the voice in my head repeats the spiritual truth I learnt from contemplative and mystic Franciscan Father Richard Rohr, who said we must:

> "Dance with our demons
> Or our Demons will
> Dance with us."

"Lacrimae rerum," wrote the poet Virgil in the immediate years before Christ. "The tears of things." *How long before my "tears of things" are dry?*

<><>

1988
'Don't You Love Me?'

I had been told in no uncertain terms at the ad briefing: 'The bastards think they own their women, and their kids.' I knew instantly it would be my toughest assignment since getting involved in social welfare.

'When his wife, or partner doesn't deliver, he knows where to move on to next. Daughters – and sons too. Their kids, fair game. Some men's idea of family is ownership. The mothers and children are their property. Part of their goods and chattels.'

Nobody ever called Gemma precious. She is of the new breed of women and is from the NSW Child Protection Council that has recently become a client of the advertising agency I part-own. Gemma has a passion and determination to right wrongs and has found a willing partner in me; I've wanted to change the world since I was a kid. We're about the same age, mid-forties, and if I am regarded as over-idealistic on occasion, this tall, large-boned, impressive woman is quixotic. Gemma is a woman of the earth; she favours the ochre colours of Australia's heart. The deep browns, greens, its rich dark red, and sometimes all at the same time. Her hair is forever tousled, she has solemn, sleepless eyes. No high heels for her, she wears sensible shoes. I have instant respect for her newfound power.

Gemma and I made a TV commercial about a father picking his little girl up from school and taking her home to an empty house. The story was all intimation of course. Coercion, the daughter reluctant to break away from her schoolmates, gets in the car, her father's driving her home, we're looking at a closed door. These words are voiced over the pictures.

'You do want to please me, don't you?'
'I promise to buy you a new bike.'

'Remember, you mustn't tell anyone about our little secret.'
'Nobody will believe you, anyway.'
'Don't make me have to hurt you.'
'Don't you love your dad?'

He had said she needed to learn, so she would know what to do when she met someone later. He said it is down to him to teach her.

He knows that, with his usual coercing, she would eventually give him what he wants.

The daughter is alone on a chair in the final scene. This message appears: "CHILD SEXUAL ASSAULT IS A CRIME.

It's Often Closer to Home than you Think:"

I only wish we could have reached out to the media with the real-life drama that had taken place at the casting session. One of the actors revealed his father had first sexually assaulted him when he was six years old; he said it was the first time he had spoken of it, and he said that 'getting it known about the bastards' would be one of the most important parts he ever played. He was very demanding of us, and under those circumstances I, for one, had no doubt: we had to honour his wish and bring him on board.

And that's the truth.

That commercial is done and dusted now. It appears on late-night television and was even picked up in the United States (with an American voice over, of course).

<>

'Fathers who molest their kids are the second lowest form of life,' Gemma says.

'Who are the first?'

'Priests. You want to hear my story?'

I pricked my ears. 'Yes, I would.'

1988
Gemma's Story

Ireland in the 1960s was ninety per cent Catholic, but the hypocritical piety that defined it was under threat. The believers were already leaving the Church, the young were full of questions about the faith that had often been beaten into them with a nun's strap, and sometimes worse, canes wielded against boys' bare arses by the priests.

And now, over twenty years later, and a strident ex-Catholic, Gemma is telling me she had come to be cognisant of the sexual satisfaction those clerics achieved in their violent acts. 'I think you know what I am saying, you were at boarding school,' she said, questioningly.

'I was.'

I am back in primary school, the fifth grade, and remembering the wild-eyed look of enjoyment on the face of our teacher who was fond of pulling our pants down and having us over his knees. 'He would be smacking our cheeks with his hand.'

'You were lucky that's all he did,' declared the social scientist.

She said her brother was not so fortunate.

'He was raped by our family priest.'

<>

'Patrick came home from school one day, crying. He told our *mam* and me that Father had told him it was time he learnt about the world. He had recently turned twelve,' she says, and pauses to relate a familiar story of a beautiful little boy, groomed to be molested; a quiet lad, who loved to sing, loved being in the choir, and helping Father on the altar. Until, one day...

And in the gloom that followed, sadness spread across Gemma's face like a darkening sky. Followed by rage. She says scornfully, 'And what do you think our mother did?'

'Our *mam*,' she says; still with love for her, she pauses the thought, while recalling her mother's piety, 'was always inviting the local priest to dinner.'

'He'd be happy to drink *dadai's* Guinness. After fecking Patrick.'

'Our mam told my brother to get himself to the bathroom and wash his mouth out with soap,' she says, lost in the terrible reminiscence.

'*Mam* said she never wanted to hear about it again,' she says ruefully. 'We weren't to tell *dadai*.'

'And that was that.' Gemma's voice broke, 'until Patrick ended it. Five years later, my brother took his own life when he jumped off a bridge and into a raging river… Where he knew he would drown… Because he had never learnt to swim,' she says, and was back there.

'Patrick was older than me. He had the eyes of an angel.'

'Can you believe our mother – in the tradition of Irish mothers – had hopes of him becoming a priest.'

'In the end, I told my father the truth of it. He didn't say much, he just nodded his head. Followed my *mam* into shame. That woman continued to go to Mass every day. The priests could do no wrong.

'Ireland was a land of denials, where the worst secrets were rarely divulged. Even when everyone knew, they kept the truth hidden. Shame held in mothers' breasts all over Ireland, while priests insinuated themselves into their families, came to dinner, took whatever fare was on offer.'

'But by then – it was immediately after Patrick's death – I had moved away, to Dublin, and university. Where, after three years, I got the degree I wanted in the social and political sciences, and I left my birth country, and the Catholic Church, for good.'

'After a while, I began writing to *mam*. I'd be telling her broken heart what a great place Australia is. The Irish "troubles" had begun by then. I told her my first impression of Sydney was unbelievable. There were no gun-toting soldiers, or bombs going off almost every day.

'My father died an alcoholic's death – the scourge of my country – and *mam* continued to exist in the one square mile of Ireland she rarely left. Her life continued to be centred on the Church, Mass every day, and food for the priest.

'Then, one day I received news that she had cancer, and her death was imminent. I made plans to make a brief return, but when the news arrived that she had gone, I cancelled.'

'I won't be going back either,' says Gemma, disdainfully and, as if requiring further justification for her decision – the Church's early mind-controlling ways always hovering – she describes a place where young Catholic girls who give birth to the bastard children of Protestant fathers often have their babies ripped away, not seen again.

'There turned out to be thousands when, in 1975, two young boys found small skeletons in County Clare. They were just the first of 9,000 babies who had been buried by nuns in eighteen places across Ireland.'

Apparently, the popular Irish President of those days, Enda Kenny, called one such gravesite a "chamber of horrors", the product of Catholic/Protestant liaisons that were described as "an inferior sub-species". Mourning the issue, he said it was customary for young pregnant girls to be thrown out of the home.

'Nothing worse for an Irish lass to be inseminated by a Protestant,' Gemma says scornfully.

'But that's enough from me. What's your story? I can see you are passionate.' Not just a greedy ad man, eh? Seems I have earned my stripes.

<><>

1958
My Story

'It was the day I *almost* lost my virginity, and one I can't forget, more than the day I did.'

'That's a story? Without a happy ending?' says Gemma and immediately apologises.

So: I set the scene, of a certain eagerness, after being cooped up in boarding school.

'Dad was a bank manager, we moved about, and he had been transferred to a town along the Murray River. It was his usual custom to find a job for me.'

'What with me being a city boy, frowned upon by the local kids, it was hard to make friends when I'd be there only for the holidays.'

'And so it was that, from Monday through Friday, I would turn up at Campbell's Winery – famous for Bobbie Burns Shiraz – where I joined the itinerant pickers there, picking the grapes at the prevailing price of 2 shillings for a basket. It was boringly laborious, but much easier than being a rouseabout, as I was once, tossing fleeces in the constant sweaty atmosphere of a shearing shed.'

'I'm struggling to describe what happened next. Without denigrating the girl, and her family. I suppose at another time, I would have said they were "lowlifes" – and they were, in a sense – but they were human beings, "life's battlers", my good-natured father would have said of them.'

'She pointed out she was 16, the same age as me, and whether that was true of her, neither of us would be considered jailbait.' (I'm hurrying to get the story out). 'We were working beside each other, on our knees among the grape vines, and I wasn't about to argue when she brushed my flies. Had she spotted my shorts were failing to disguise the tell-tale bulge that had arrived?'

'Earlier, when we had gravitated together, I discovered sex begins with a lot of talking. The family wasn't "cultured", as I often heard a prejudiced aunt say, but she was nice, and she liked me. She said so anyway. It seemed they were often on the move, chasing the ripening fruit throughout the season, professional pickers.'

'Day's end had arrived not before time and, with her parents heading off to the pub, we'd be alone for the next hour, at least, she said, and guided me past the vines and to a thicket of willows by a slow running creek. I thought it was an ideal spot. But she wasn't looking for romance.'

(Wary about the next bit, I am red-faced and pause before continuing): 'She dropped her pants, just like that, and I was about to follow suit when she pointed to the bulge in her belly. How could I have missed that?'

'"Do you think it matters?" she asked, and that was when I died for the first time in my upbringing.'

Confessing I knew I wasn't going to do it then, I say to Gemma, 'All my sorrow was suddenly one-sided, all for that girl.'

'Anyway, she told me her mother knew of someone in the next town, "who would get rid of it". Just like that, as though the abortion would be no more than a service call.'

'Did she tell you who the father was?' Gemma asks.

My eyes filled with water. Gemma already knew. 'Well, that's the part I prefer to forget. She said her father often came home from the pub looking to satisfy his lust, and sometimes she was "it".'

'I'm so sorry.'

'It's alright,' I say, and supposed losing the desire for the girl so abruptly was a lesson in sex that I didn't want to know. 'Not at not-so sweet sixteen. I think it was when I discovered education is the most important thing in the world.'

'And when the subject of girls came up at school, as it often did among us sex-starved boarders, I was told I had been lucky.' While others ribbed me – 'You could have been a father!' – Maurice from New Caledonia was the most advanced among us, being French, the frogs are always at it – and he said it was a clear-cut case: the young woman – "*jeune femme*" – 'was looking for someone to *claim* as the father'.

'But I still have the memory of her being told that if she didn't deliver, she'd cop a punch.'

<><>

1988
'The Murder of the Soul'

Gemma has a new brief: from Canberra, a new Women's Unit; apparently, we are about to meet a group of violent men who, while they rape women, are happy to beat up the "rock spiders". Seems that in the jail's pecking order, child molesters are the lowest form of life.

<>

You can't judge a book by its cover.

There are six men in green prison garb, of various sizes, overweight, underweight. Two standouts, one muscled up from hours in the gym, a snake tattoo along one arm, sauntering arrogantly, the other small and slight, who couldn't blow out a candle; his eyes dart about nervously. They are accompanied by two guards and while we can see them all, we are unseen ourselves behind a one-way mirror. We had been urged to remain quiet; one cough and with their suspicions realised, some may clam up. As it is, I am told they had grasped the opportunity to be let out for a day, to be in touch with the "outside" that they missed.

Or was it something else? I dare to speculate: had they, like Hamlet, found "conscience had made cowards" of them, after all? They appear to be an ordinary bunch, they could be anywhere, and I can see that could be a problem when they came before the law. The violence they had committed was not readily apparent; appearances can be deceptive. We're here to listen to build a message that would resonate with a target audience of everyone in Australia for our ad. (What's wrong with the world when we must tell people *rape* is a *crime*? That thought I will take to my grave).

The presider, a psychologist, male, has positioned himself at the table's head; Gemma, beside me, is seething; she knows she has to accept there is no way these men will open up to a woman.

He begins to tease out the rapists' stories, and we are soon educated. Here is what was said, in those men's own words:

'When I get home from the pub, I expect a decent feed and a root, and she's in trouble if I don't look like getting both, in that order.'

'Yeah, sometimes you gotta rough 'em up a bit to get what you want.'

'It's a man's right, and her obligation. What she signed up for.'

'In my book, my woman's place is in the kitchen or on her back.'

'What did she expect when she was dressed like a tart?'

'She was a prick teaser, coming on to me.'

'Deserved what she fucking got.'

With that, they, themselves, had written the line that became the focus of black and white posters along bus sides, at airports, and other strategic places across Australia:

IT'S A CRIME. NO ONE EVER DESERVES TO BE RAPED.

<>

It had been a tough day at the office, and we were left with this choice piece of dialogue delivered by one of them, pointedly directed at the mirror that we thought had concealed us from their stares.

'Tell them.' (Staring hard at us, on the other side of the one-way glass).

'Tell 'em – why don't you? – you pathetic prick of a human being.' (He gave a nasal snarl that gave every impression he was going to deck the man).

'Tell 'em how you had a knife at her throat while you struggled to get that joke of a cock of yours out of your fucking spunk-stained underpants.'

Even in rape, there's a pecking order of things. Rape is as old as history and while history may have a habit of repeating itself, the time for change had been set.

<>

Fifteen years later, with the law toughened, two young boys will be incarcerated for a series of gang rapes committed across Sydney, over a short space of time, before their hideous rampage was curtailed.

They called their terrified victims 'sluts'. But justice caught up with them, and they were handed sentences of 32 years and 55 years respectively, to shouts in the court by onlookers hoping they 'rot in Hell'.

So many young lives changed, but none more so than the girls they chose to have their evil pleasure with. It's forever in their souls.

Neither boy had shown remorse.

Psychologist Jeff Bond says in the game of rugby league, gang rape is as commonplace as binge drinking.

"The sharing of women is a bit pervasive and has developed over time. The culture that surrounds some clubs is wrong and it provides a platform for sex and violence. Clubs protect players. It is treated as 'boys being boys' and there is a cone of protection and silence."

The Sydney Morning Herald, "What Dogs do" – 24 February 2004

<><><>

Two
MAXIMA CULPA

2014
Nothing But the Truth

He is conservatively dressed, inconspicuous in a fawn suit and matching tie, a beige man, some would say; but his blandness should not deceive. He is, though small in stature, far from a crudely warlike Napoleonic figure, except in one respect: he is a man of tactics, big of mind.

Possessed of a certain quiet arrogance, he is determined to get through his first appearance at the Royal Commission into Institutional Child Sexual Abuse without damage to the Church.

It is a sunny day, with intermittent clouds casting their occasional shadows upon the building. Earlier, at the break of dawn in fact, a small group of survivors had taken up their usual position at the court's entrance, lest they miss the sought-after seats in the public gallery; they are filing in now, along with the eager media. It has been almost two years since the Inquiry began and the mood of silent anger inside the court has not diminished.

The one-time Provincial of the Marists, a teaching Order that has a 200-year heritage, has been a big catch. Some are already saying it is the Catholic Church that is on trial here; and, like the other institutions that are forced to have their day in court, it is fighting for its very existence.

He knows the stakes have never been higher, but he hopes his version of the truth will be enough to evoke sympathy for the many good men who had once been under his tutelage before his retirement and, as far as he is aware, did not stray. Many have left the Marist Brothers since, including one of its most remarkable headmasters, a friend, who, in a portent for Catholicism's future, is now happily married to the woman he had long loved.

But now the Marist leader is just another man in the dock. Summoning all his defences, he tells himself he will face his inquisitor with the strength that comes from a personal conviction – that what had happened is but a blip in his coveted Order that the world will soon get over.

He secretly knows that, like the Holocaust, the world won't forget.

Meanwhile, the memories he has of many fallen men, the ones he had attempted to change their terrible ways – their evil acts that he still fails to understand – hadn't he urged them to confess their sins to the God of redemption?

The Marists had been 2,000-strong during his time at the top; although less now, its presence remains and there are parents still sending their children to its schools.

These terrible times will pass, and now it's his task to save the Order from itself.

A tiny bead of moisture appears upon his forehead and slowly edges down; he rescues it with a tissue from a box that had been discreetly placed near at hand and prepares himself to parry the questioning. Curiously angry at the position he has found himself in, he has been asking himself: *Why should I be on trial?*

All these years later, and he still believes the rape of a child is a momentary lapse: a "kiddy-fiddling" that he had been told by some "experts" the Church had introduced him to is curable.

And anyway, the kids would get over it; "time heals all wounds". *God understands.*

He prepares himself for the worst, as his steely-eyed adversary approaches her post, pauses, and is set to begin.

He is not used to facing a woman of power. It's fair to assume he quietly resents it.

<>

Counsel Assisting Gail Furness is a formidable figure; slight, like the man before her, she has, like him, always dressed conservatively in her job as a prosecutor. Tailored pastel suits her choice, with a simple pearl necklace, her hair on the short side; all of which draws attention away from her, as well-trained in the forensic art of cross-examination, Gail Furness maintains a devastating calmness and will be constantly probing – killer-lawyer that she is.

Furness is presently unaware that the succession of clerics that come before her penetrating gaze will be preparation for the day when she will find herself questioning one of the world's most dangerous hierarchs, whom many already believe to be a danger to the Catholic Church and the Pope himself, Cardinal George Pell.

Counsel Assisting Furness will be on her mettle for as long as it takes to get to the truth, and truth will out people, it always does.

She has been with the Inquiry since the beginning; she ought to be tired of it all, but will stick with it until the end. That she is in it for the duration is evidenced by the way she focuses her eagle eyes on the man before her now, who, like so many others, has covered up crimes against children.

Over two long days, she aims to calmly draw out those crimes.

<>

'Within a very short space of time, Brother Gregory Sutton was out of the country and in therapy in Canada, am I correct, Brother?'

The Marist leader stirs, before informing the court it had been over two decades since he had been Provincial, and his memory has grown dim (*Why so? I marvel. Mine hasn't. Of that day he compromised me*) – and without batting an eye.

But denial won't keep him safe. He is asked why he had sent a 'known *paedophile*' – known by him – away to 'avoid the law'.

He did not see it that way.

'Wasn't it "excessive haste"?'

No, he had been 'trying to get him through to intensive therapy, I think you could say'.

'No, Brother, it was to avoid a scandal.'

Furness spelt out the circumstances to the court. Sutton had undergone two unsuccessful attempts at counselling in Sydney and Melbourne, before being sent to the Southdown Institute in Canada, where, out of sight, out of mind, it had 'experience with sexual abusers.'

He is unperturbed: 'The Melbourne therapist said he was "unable to work with this man. He does not have sufficient self-awareness to be able to proceed through therapy with me," he said.'

But it won't be enough to sway anyone; no matter how it is couched, the simple fact of the matter, Furness says, 'is that a man who was later convicted of multiple crimes against the children in his care had, in the six-year interval between freedom and court been swept away in a figurative "dead of night" scenario before he was discovered and forcibly brought back.'

The law is long, and we learn that in 1996, serial paedophile Brother Gregory Sutton was finally convicted on 67 counts of the molestation of children. It begged the question: how had this been allowed to take place? And how many young ones could have been saved if the Church had done the right thing and handed him over to the law?

Sutton was sentenced to 18 years' incarceration; he served 12 and in 2008 was returned to the community.

His one-time Marist leader rejects claims that he had frustrated police efforts to track his fiendish colleague down.

But he is soon forced to admit to the hushed court room that he 'first became aware Sutton had abused a student in 1989.'

And how had he learnt that? His shoulders drop noticeably, along with his eyes. He faces the Commissioner, who has often been impatient to hear the answers.

'When a former student of Sutton's at a North Queensland school committed suicide,' he says to a suddenly hushed court.

(We can be reminded that the inevitable stain on the Catholic Church had already seen 12 boys end their lives by their own hands in the Victorian town of Ballarat, the home to several child-molesting priests, and one-time domicile of then-priest, George Pell and his lifelong friend, who he will support, ironically, through thick and thin in the courts of justice – the notorious serial rapist, Father Gerald Ridsdale.)

And so, the relentlessly determined questioning continues, and in one astounding moment, the one-time Marist leader loses his way when he says to the court he would have to seek 'specialist advice' if it was 'criminal for an adult to masturbate a child or demand to be touched on the genitals'.

But there are more revelations to come.

<>

Returned to the witness box the following day, the defender of the Marists is being asked to explain how he had dealt with 'serial paedophile, Brother John'.

Known in the court records also by his birth name, Kostka Chute, the Inquiry is informed the infamous abuser 'had molested 39 children between 1976 and 1990.'

He finally faced the law in 2008 when he was convicted of multiple counts of molesting boys – and sentenced to just *two years* jail.

The Inquiry is now informed that Brother John/Chute had served at 12 Marist schools over the previous four decades.

Equally challenging for the Marist on the spot is that the paedophile register, Broken Rites, declares on its website that after a boy reported that Brother John had indecently assaulted him, 'the Head of the Province flew to Canberra to investigate but Chute was allowed to continue teaching'.

Then, things grew to be much worse for the Marists when a second Canberra boy reported that he had been sexually abused by the Marist's compulsive *paedophile* Brother.

But it turns out that it wasn't until the latest matter was taken directly to the head of the Order that Chute was finally withdrawn from the school. Early January 1994 saw Brother John/Chute no longer working as a teacher.

What happened then? 'He was transferred to the Marist training centre in Dundas, Sydney and then, in 1997, to the Marist Farmhouse at Mittagong in southern NSW.'

Where he would be safe?

'The Marist authorities managed to prevent these complaints from reaching the police,' the eagle-eyed Counsel told the court.

<>

But the law wasn't done with the man I had once known as a spiritual adviser and was happy to call a friend.

After his Sydney appearance, he is called before the Commission's Newcastle sittings.

Where, with more probing, it is revealed that in his time as Marist leader, he had had 'several more Brothers admit they had been molesting children'.

'How many, Brother, how many?' asks Counsel Assisting Furness.

Despite prosecutor and witness knowing one another well by now, the answer to that question will be like getting blood out of a stone.

'Was it two?'

'More than two.'

'Was it ten?'

'No, more than ten.'

He would have to check.

And so, it is 48 hours later that the Commission hears the stunning news that over 150 men of the Marist Order had been accused of sexually assaulting children in its care.

'Name them,' says the steely-eyed Counsel.

'You will bring that list of 150 Brothers to this court on Monday,' she repeats. 'We'd like all of them please, Brother.'

<>

What's in a name?

Meaningful pseudonyms are common among the clerics of the Catholic Church, and while "Jesus" proliferates in the Latin countries such as Spain and much of South America, it is rare to be called after the Lord's name in Australia, where, as in Europe and the United States, many adopt the names of the saints instead. The entire register of Jesus' apostles – Matthew, Mark, Luke and John – are common names all over Australia.

Literature abounds with names that often prove to be ironic (for example, my parents named my younger brother, David, and one day he would need every ounce of the boy with the slingshot's strength to slay the "Goliath" that had drawn him into a destructive religious cult).

But the Marist leader, a singular man, secure in his own skin, was to adopt the pseudonym Alexis, a 4th-century Roman nobleman who had converted to Christianity; his chosen name meant *"defender and protector"*.

What's in a name?

<><>

2023
My Worst Nightmare

This book began with a lie when my initiation into Catholic Church criminality was to be secretly asked to engage in the cover-up of clerical sex crimes against children in its care.

Reflecting now upon those times of the early 1990s, I remember the Marist in charge of my youngest son's dorm as being tall, with vacant, suspicious eyes, a pock-marked face, and not particularly outgoing. I don't recall us ever engaging in much conversation.

Brother Ross wasn't easily approachable and even his own attempts to reach out seemed to get lost on the way. I thought many of the Brothers had a sense of inferiority and he came across as a good example. I thought he was a lonely figure who lacked warmth and was always on the edges.

I had only been a Catholic for fifteen years and had never accepted the idea of celibacy – that I believe is against nature, despite being constantly handed the Catholic mantra that living without sexual intimacy is a "gift" from Jesus' cross.

By 1991, the Brotherhood was already declining in Marist schools, and I wasn't surprised that the isolation imposed on clerics in religious institutions, the enforced loneliness, and separateness from we mere mortals, was having its effect (many clerics are believed to have "secret marriages", often with nuns (despite the nuns' Superiors insisting they avert their eyes whenever a man approaches).

But I wasn't prepared for the Catholic Church's curse to hit me square in the face when, upon learning decades after our youngest son had spent his first year at Sydney elite boarding school, St Joseph's College, that he had been under the "care" of a paedophile. One who was so adept at concealing his crimes that, although two classmates of our son had left the college under suspicious circumstances (apparently, "Joey's was not suitable", and in the other case, it was after being "bullied"), none of them were aware that it was anything more.

Brother Ross Francis Murrin – a criminal's full name is always spelt out in the courts – first came to my attention this year, when, like a bolt of lightning searing my soul, I learnt he had been arraigned as a child rapist, his criminal activities going back years.

In one of four subsequent trials for the abuse of children in his care, Murrin had pleaded guilty to 17 charges – the offences taking place at his first school in Sydney's western suburbs in 1974.

The then 51-year-old was sentenced under an outdated law at the time of his crimes when sentences for such "offences" – as they were referred to then, rather than "crimes" – ranged from non-custodial to a maximum of (only) three-and-a-half years.

In 1974, Murrin was barely 18 and, with little teacher training, was placed in charge of boys barely 5–6 years younger. It seems even the law of that time failed to recognise child molestation as *rape*, and the common law was joined at the hip with institutions such as the Marist Brothers – that, we know now, saw the raping of our "little ones" (Pope Francis' description) as little more than *kiddy-fiddling*.

None of the many stories – the world knows they are in multiples of thousands – of sexual abuse of children by Catholic clerics has affected me as deeply and personally as that of Brother Ross Murrin.

While I was ignorant of the monster presiding over the 1991 intake of new boys away from their homes boarding at Sydney's esteemed St Joseph's College, I had met the Provincial (head) of the Marists who had sought my help in covering up some of the terrible acts fiends such as Brother Ross – as known by the classes he presided over, the affectionate nomenclature extending to us, the parents – was already famous for.

I had run away from the Marist leader's request in dismay and astonishment – we had often been happy for him to share a meal with our family – and here I am, this book prompted initially by the effect our meeting had on me that day – remembering the rose bushes lining the path to the Marist headquarters. Metaphorically, they told lies to those who bent to smell their exquisite fragrance, but I had grasped their thorny stems – Spike Milligan's *The New Rose* – the effect that has had on my life is immense: I have nightmares, during which I am often railing against monsters.

Such as, it turns out, Brother Ross Murrin.

The institutional Catholic Church has lost me, and I am hanging onto my faith by a thread, thanks to a community of like-minded followers of Catholic Christianity that is intent on recreating the original Jesus Church.

I owe my gratitude to all of them.

Yet all the while I am driven further into the mire, writing about the wider evil that has become synonymous with the Catholic Church, and all it stands for.

<>

The investigative site *Broken Rites* has made an exhaustive investigation into the abuse career of Brother Ross Murrin and has traversed Australia in following his career.

Ross Murrin joined the Marist Order in 1973, aged 17. One year later, with no real education training, he had been put in charge of 35 primary school boys.

A surprise to many, *Broken Rites* has found the abuse began immediately and the next three decades saw Murrin being moved on by the Church in its customary way, facilitating him with opportunities to abuse at eleven colleges and schools from Sydney to Brisbane and far North Queensland.

Tellingly, Murrin spent only one-to-three years in any one place, and even was located for some years in Rome (the Vatican State a safe haven, like the places, in faraway isolated sites, where ostensibly there for their "health", the Church's monsters avoid the law of their lands).

Murrin was a multiple offender who knew what he was doing was wrong, and he may have sought out the Marist Brotherhood, where, like a lion seeking out prey, a smorgasbord of opportunity lay.

And feast he did: Jason Parkinson is a lawyer who represented two siblings who had both been molested by the criminal Brother in the boys' North Queensland school.

'During the 1970s and 80s, the religious Brothers in boarding schools had more power over the children than their parents did,' says Parkinson.

'To repeatedly give paedophiles access to children in that setting is reckless and reprehensible.'

Amazingly, Murrin's lawyer in the 2008 case – paid by the Marist Order? – asked Judge Helen Murrell to accept there was 'mitigating evidence' from a psychiatrist, wanting the court to believe his client 'had fallen victim to a system (that had been) very slow to respond to this nature of sexual abuse'.

(*Broken Rites* sees it as 'an admission from the Marists that the Order was negligent in turning Murrin loose upon young boys'.)

<>

The dossier of Murrin's crimes committed upon children are in the multiples; the list is detailed on *Broken Rites* and it beggars belief on two counts; one, that Murrin's offending was so brazen, often being in broad daylight with other children witnessing; two, it is certainly questionable that the Marists wouldn't have known about the fiend in their midst.

The 2008 court was told: 'The abuse often took place when Murrin ordered a boy to come to his desk and sit on his lap, when he would maul the boy sexually in front of the rest of the class.'

On other occasions, 'a pupil would witness another pupil being assaulted'.

Assaults often occurred on 'religious retreats' and during detentions, when Murrin had the boy at his mercy, on his own.

Murrin 'abused a boy in a nearby room, while his colleagues were in the library, watching a film'.

Broken Rites describes the Marist Brother "pulling a boy's pants down from behind, pinning him to the ground".

<>

Brother Ross Murrin was seen to be a formidable figure at this time.

The presider in the 2008 case, Judge Murrell described Murrin: 'Even at 18 (he) was tall…the victims were intimidated by the status and size of the offender.'

Frightened to speak out, victims had been compelled to silence.

But when eight came forward with sworn statements 30 years later, the police said they expected there to be many more and after the 2008 sentencing, two years later Murrin was further sentenced on crimes ranging from the rape of six boys to acts of indecency.

Returned to court twice more, Murrin's final appearance in 2020 saw his lawyers argue successfully for a non-custodial sentence, in order, as the judge in the trial determined, for the paedophile 'to care for his 94-year-old father'.

Brother Ross Murrin may have raped up to 100 boys over the course of his molesting career, most around age 10, and at least one had perished in a drug overdose, aged 22, forcing his conscience-stricken friend – who had, unbelievably, witnessed the abuses, as so often occurred in Murrin's rapes – to come forward with the story.

While unusual for victims to tell their parents, the court was told of two siblings whose father had rushed from their home in the Queensland outback, only to learn that the school headmaster had given the boys tickets to the circus in return for keeping such a serious matter quiet.

Both Murrin and the headmaster were moved to other schools.

Murrin's entry in *Broken Rites* runs to five pages, where I learnt the Marist had unwittingly incriminated himself when he wrote a letter of apology to both the parents of one boy he had serially molested, even after leaving school, and to his Provincial.

Whether the Marist leader handed the letter to the police is not clear, but victims' lawyers were quick to subpoena it as an admission of guilt.

Upon sentencing, Judge Murrell said: 'The Marist Brothers were negligent in inflicting Murrin upon his students, especially when the Marists were transferring him (as a known offender) to more schools.'

'Our belief has been rocked in all things Catholic,' said a boy's father.

Murrin's first trial had seen the judge decry that her hands had been tied by the 1970s' "rap over the knuckles" law that applied to "crimes of this type", but Judge Helen Murrell had given some comfort when she informed the court: 'Since then, things have changed, and the community has come to understand that authority figures, even religious authority figures, are not immune from such conduct.'

Brother Ross Murrin was a serial rapist and those who knew best had spent so much time and money avoiding justice for his myriad victims.

The Marist Brothers are well-endowed to provide compensation: while one of Australia's largest property owners, the Order is a standout shareholder on the register of many Australasian companies, and others worldwide.

Why would the Marists place all this in jeopardy by helping criminals avoid the law?

<> <>

2000
Rock Spider!

Whack!

'Take that, *cunt*! And be quiet, or I might be forced to break a bone.'

He lays a good punch right in the solar plexus; the hated paedophile grimaces in pain and dutifully obeys the command. He knows the pair are deadly serious; the one doing all the talking is the older of the two, works out every spare moment in the prison gym, and now, his tattoos stretching, he is pinning the new arrival's arms behind his back, and inviting his young accomplice to take over.

'You have a crack, and don't be a pansy, your first is always the hardest.'

He glances at the guards, who have given the nod, and catches the hint of their faint, approving smiles.

'And keep away from the cunt's head,' he says, wryly. 'That could make it tough for everyone,' followed by a nod to their "audience" – of two.

The senior of the prison guards raises a hand in acknowledgement; both he and his younger partner are keen to see rough justice applied to the jail's lowest level of "crim". The former takes over.

Whack!

Turns out it is an extremely good hit and, with a rush of air, the recipient crumples in a heap and falls to the ground.

His punishers have him exactly where they want him, and the kicking commences.

Shoe leather on flesh makes a deadening sound, and as far as all who are there for the hiding are concerned, he who had once dared to degrade humanity – and 'to fuck with children' – has gotten his just deserts.

The child molester is soon a whimpering mess, lying on the floor while the guards wait for him to get to his feet by himself, and return to the "rock" he lives under, in a jail that is ill-equipped to deal with the lowest class of human being.

The first-timer gazes down at him, and quietly observes the pair of prison guards, who are continuing their indifference.

'We oughtn't to be put in the same jail as lowlifes like him,' he says pointedly.

'I'll go along with that,' says the elder of the guards.

'People have been known to die round these parts,' he says directly to the frightened face of the hated *rock spider*, who has dragged himself to his feet and hopes for the safety of his cell anytime soon.

Later, the younger of the pair of prison guards, who is not hardened yet, will be more understanding, although circumspect. 'There's got to be a place for the likes of him, for his own safety,' he will reiterate.

Everyone in the guards' room agreed that it is not to be found 'anywhere here'.

<><>

2000
In the Middle of Nowhere

Junee is a sleepy haven, located 850 kilometres from Sydney and 496 kilometres from Melbourne. Once a major rail hub – before diesel superseded steam – the Junee Roundhouse, now defunct, is Australia's largest, its huge overhead water tank left to rust. Junee's streets are lined with grand hotels and impressive government buildings that had arrived with the 1890s' gold rush, when 10,000 punters were drawn to try their luck.

One hundred years later, job-losses had cut the Junee population by three-quarters.

But the geography of the town's isolation soon attracted government eyes, and in 1993 the Junee Correctional Centre became a reality on the edge of town.

Costing $53 million, this special prison can house up to 1,200 offenders; about half are incarcerated for sex crimes. The jail incorporates 480 maximum security beds, employs some 200 locals, and has quietly become a major financial asset to the once-thriving town.

One criminal priest there said, through a third party, he couldn't help himself when he was drunk. Serving a 20-year sentence for multiple child-sex offences, he has sworn off the grog and says Mass every day for other prisoners. Weet-Bix is used for the host, while milk substitutes for the wine.

Meanwhile, in one of life's great ironies, the Junee website invites ordinary folk to enjoy "An Ideal Weekend for a Lifelong Escape".

The Junee Correctional Centre is a serious endeavour, aimed in the modern sense to be as much about punishment as compassion and rehabilitation. The year 2000 saw a mild-mannered psychiatrist contracted by the Junee facility's management "to evaluate a *NETT program…for a group of inmates" at the jail. Led by eminent psychiatrist Doctor Robert Gordon, the rest of his group comprised a distinguished lawyer, a psychologist, and a senior researcher, all conversant with the scourge of *paedophilia*. (*Normalisation, Education, Training and Treatment.)

The *Junee Study* involved two groups of 18 child sex offenders who were examined over a 17-week period. Doctor Gordon told me he was not surprised that there was no shortage of volunteers: all human beings seek 'a community of others', he says.

The document is not easy reading.

"Empathy training, sex offenders and re-offending: The problem of high re-offence rates by sex offenders upon release."

"In order to even begin an empathic process, an individual needs to have the ability to recognise emotions in others."

"The social cues of fear and terror that elicit pro-social actions from most people appear to be ignored by sexual offenders. These emotion cues are transmitted most clearly by the face."

The above are my *italics*, and what is written there reminds me of my own experience when, in 1989, I had been contracted to the NSW Child Protection Council, where I was privy to child sex offenders talking about 'the urge that can't be stopped'.

'It's the way God made me...they enjoy it, as much as I do, I know they do,' more than one admitted.

'*Alexithymia*, that's what we have named it, means lack of emotion. An inability to read the face. From the Greek,' explains Dr Robert Gordon MBBS, DPM FRANZCP, as he gazes at me sympathetically and with a certain reassurance: 'a is "lack", lexis is "word"; *thymos* "emotions".'

'That lack of empathy is not confined to child molesters,' says the eminent psychiatrist. 'Unfortunately, some of their protectors may not be immune to this psychopathic condition.'

<>

"CAN THE CHURCH BE SAVED?" asks the cover of *Time* in April 2002.

"Why Do They Target Kids?" the lead story asks, and goes on to quote a Seattle doctor, versed in the field: 'The true hard-core pedophile *(American spelling)* is drawn to children not merely incidentally but exclusively (and) seems to target same-sex and opposite sex children equally.'

'Overwhelmingly, abusers appear to be male. We have been waiting for the avalanche of women offenders to appear. We're still waiting.'

<><>

2012
An Extraordinary Woman in the Top Job

It had been a long winter of discontent when Australia's first woman Prime Minister, and lawyer, Julia Gillard, established a *Royal Commission into Institutional Responses to Child Sexual Abuse*; its report would be wide-ranging and take five years; it was an achievement that achieved bipartisan support.

Earlier, Prime Minister Gillard had given the famous 'Misogyny Speech', in the Parliament in response to accusations of sexism made against her by then Opposition leader, the conservative Catholic, Tony Abbott.

The Royal Commission initiative would define the Gillard Labor government and have real consequences for the safety of women and children in Australia and the wider world, prompting, in part, Pope Francis to have the Vatican conduct its own investigations into child sexual assault in his Church (where he would not be prepared for some of the worst offenders being those nearest him, including bishops and cardinals).

Nine years later, the new Pope's initiative would come to ensnare his predecessor. Pope Benedict XVI would be 94 and retired (the first pope to resign in 600 years), when in January 2022 the Catholic Church would report that while Archbishop of Munich and Freising (1977–82) as the then clerical hierarch, Joseph Ratzinger (the birth name by which Pope Benedict XVI was still known at the time) not only "knew" that several of his priests were child abusers but was happy to allow them to continue in their posts, many as parish priests.

Under the headline 'Vatican to study abuse report that faults Pope Benedict', the January 20 issue of *America Online* would report German lawyer Martin Pusch as saying that Benedict's "claiming ignorance...is not reconcilable with the files".

Followers of the brilliant fictional film *The Two Popes* will recall Anthony Hopkins as Benedict, sitting at his desk strewn with reports he had denied justice.

<>

Our future is ultimately in the hands of those with power, and times had changed; finally, a woman would lead Australia.

But the Catholic Church was tragically out of step in a changed world.

Even under the more merciful Francis, who many of us from my small congregation have defined as 'remarkable', the male-dominated Vatican remains seemingly unperturbed.

The Church is losing people *en masse*, as the horrific revelations of its greatest betrayal since those early traitors conspired to kill God, took root.

'They know not what they do,' Jesus said at the time.

The last word had fallen to a woman then – when Pilate's wife gave solemn warning that she had had a frightening dream about the man people were already calling the "Christ".

Governor Pontius Pilate had washed his hands of the gravest matter he would ever have to deal with; washed them of this strange, charismatic rebel whose popularity was growing by the day. The marriage between the most powerful couple in Judea was destined never to be the same again.

It was Prime Minister Gillard who was the first leader in the world to recognise the widespread betrayal of the nation's children as crimes against humanity that must no longer go unpunished.

Justice for the massive caseload of victims has been a long time coming, and Gillard's government has vowed all child victims of sexual abuse within Institutions will also be recompensed for their pain.

I, like many others, have been waiting, and not without fear and trepidation, for this day; it is 24 years since the auspicious meeting that changed my life in the Catholic Church, fed into my conscience where it has languished, only to surface on occasion and play havoc with my psyche.

But now it's time: the one-time Marist leader is about to have his day in court; and I will follow the transcript of those eagerly-awaited proceedings – in the hope they will set me free – free to tell my part in this horrific story, once and for all.

Sometime in the legendary 1960s I read Elizabeth Smart's *By Grand Central Station I Sat Down and Wept* and, somehow – strange the tricks our minds play – it is easy to see why that outpouring of grief resonates with me now.

<>

'Australians won't tolerate further inaction on child abuse,' Prime Minister Julia Gillard is saying about the almighty Act that has seen the emergence of the *Royal Commission into Institutional Responses to Child Sexual Abuse*. It is the eleventh of November, already a date of both celebration for all, and infamy for others, signifying the end of the War in Europe 67 years previously; and in 1975 the game-changing Labor government of Prime Minister Gough Whitlam was unceremoniously dismissed by the Governor General at the time, John Kerr.

Now with the Gillard initiative, one of the most important dates in Australia's history has joined the end of the First World War as being a day of hope and justice for those victims of despicable crimes – the nation's children and their families.

It would fall to a steely-eyed prosecutor with consummate determination to continue her work and prize open the vast litany of horror stories the Church had been secretly keeping and pave the way for survivors of abuse by its clerics to make their cases to receive compensation.

Priests have certain powers in the Church and the percentage of Catholic priests molesting children would be revealed to be up to 100 times higher than in the wider world.

But, in 1989, the notion that a priest would rape a child was a secret held by both the Churches and in the bosom of parents, who felt shame had been brought upon their families, for all time.

The greatest betrayal in the history of Catholicism would come to be seen for what it is: a slap in the very face of God.

One that would claim thousands of priests, numerous pharisaical hierarchs, and continue to deplete the Church's vast wealth well into the future.

As the mass exodus of people voting with their feet continues, Catholicism would become the "smaller Church", promised as long ago as 1967, by a lowly German priest, Joseph Ratzinger, who was being said at the time to be "an intellectual force in the Catholic Church", and would become pope.

But, as Benedict XVI, he would prove to be no man of the people and, crushed by the revelations of sexual abuse by priests, the first pope in 600 years to resign his post.

Always the traditionalist, he would issue his resignation in Latin.

"The only thing necessary for the triumph of evil is for good men to do nothing," said the 19th-century philosopher, John Stuart Mill. Words I once saw echoed by a Holocaust survivor in the Schindler Museum in Krakow, they have stayed with me and came to drive me to write this book. If one *knows*, one has an obligation.

<>

Meanwhile, in a valley, miles from nowhere, in the Canadian wilds, languish some of the Catholic Church's worst child molesters; there, ostensibly, to be "changed", when they would be returned to normal duties among the children they crave.

Many were sent there by that august institution, the Marist Brothers; out of sight in that secret place, they are never out of mind to the hurt and aggrieved.

<><>

2016
Blind Rage!

Ian Lawther is telling me he had never felt angrier and hopes he never will again; he had been in a rage for weeks. We are talking over the phone, thanks to my brother who works in the care industry under the newly formed National Disability Insurance Scheme (NDIS). David wanted me to check in with one of his clients who has a story to tell 'that will be of special interest to your book'.

Ian says he hadn't been sleeping; his thoughts filled with murderous intent. It didn't help having a wife who had been brought up a staunch Catholic. But ever since learning why their son had been self-harming, he was keeping much of the worst of it to himself. Stephen was 17 years old when, after fighting the shame and hurt of his early teenage years, he told his father their local priest had been serially abusing him and others for years – because, as a man of God, it seemed he was super-human and could.

The priest, David Daniel, had begun abusing the boy from age 10; this made it personal, very personal. When Ian had married Pam, he had signed up to protect his family at all costs; not for him any more talking with bishops, there'd be no protracted court battle – always doomed to fail, with the Church protecting its own. Daniel's fate was sealed: justice was to be Ian Lawther's and it had to be quick.

Ian Lawther had never wanted to kill before, but now he was going to murder a priest.

He knew where Daniel's latest post was; he had been tracking him for a long time. He couldn't stomach that his boy's abuser would be saying Mass there, baptising children, celebrating marriages, hearing confessions, and all part of his job while he groomed his next victim; until the Catholic Church would move him on, leaving a trail of accusations and innuendo behind.

How was he going kill him?

Shooting him would be too easy, too impersonal. Ian Lawther needed to witness the fear and shame in the priest's eyes.

Anyway, Ian didn't own a gun.

As a peace-loving man, he wouldn't use it on another human being if he did.

He could run the 'bastard' over, but that would also be too impersonal, too quick.

Ian needed to lock Father David Daniel's eyes with his.

He would kill the priest who had abused his son – with *his bare hands*.

'I wanted to get my hands around his neck and squeeze until he went still. I did what I thought any man would think of doing, given the circumstances. Given the temporary loss of my mind.'

He climbed into his car, started it up, and prepared to head out of the driveway.

<>

But it wasn't going to turn out the way he had planned. Ian's hands froze on the wheel – 'the pain was unimaginable' – and blood vessels burst behind his left eye. And today – it is some 16 years later – the man I am talking to is technically blind.

But he needs to talk. What happened to the priest? He says the law finally caught up with Father David Daniel, and in the year 2000, the priest who had sexually abused his son was finally charged and sentenced to just six years jail, with parole set at four years and six months. Prompting the cry from the bleachers: 'Should have got life!'

Especially considering the police had located six victims: four boys, a girl, and an adult male.

David Daniel, Catholic priest, had faced 18 counts of abuse, molesting one of his victims for four long, horrific years, while another had been in his evil clutches for an unbelievable, unconscionable 16 years.

While his victims will live in Hell, Daniel will go on to die quietly in his own space, aged 79.

But the serial abuser's death remains of little comfort to those devastated by Father David Daniel's crimes, and the silent inaction of the Catholic Church.

Ian says the Catholic Church 'ruined his family'. He and wife, Pam, had trusted the Church to do 'the right and proper thing'; but, like so many other victims, it had failed them.

He had taken their son's case to the Church hierarchy where he was met with the usual disbelieving silence that is happening all over the world to those seeking justice: the Catholic Church is deaf to the most terrible of truths, continuing to fall back on its desire to protect itself – no matter the cost.

Angry and aggrieved – but not to be deterred – Ian wrote to the Vatican. His plea received more silence.

But that wasn't going to be the end of it for the determined father of a son who had been irreparably damaged after being sexually abused on multiple occasions by one of its priests.

Delving further, Ian discovered that the Church had known Father David Daniel was a paedophile for some time.

He was told it had been aware of his crimes for at least five years and, in all probability, went as far back as Daniel's time in the seminary.

It was damning evidence, a monstrous cover-up.

And it had turned a gentle, patient, loving man of great, inspiring talent as an acclaimed master craftsman and builder into the rage that would take away his livelihood and change Ian's attitude to the Church forever.

We must meet in the flesh. I fly to Melbourne where I will have my brother for company.

<><>

2019
A True Saint

We are winding our way up a pebbled driveway, past native shrubs lovingly planted, the air scented with eucalyptus; native flowers, the humming of bees signalling the arrival of spring.

Home to the Lawthers is a fairy-tale cottage; it just missed the 2009 fires and still dares the bush. It has a great view sitting on a hill is made of mudbrick and rammed earth, has a corrugated iron roof, and hand-made bricks on the floor; it is home just for Ian and his wife now. Pam's dream home. Built to her design by her husband's careful hands.

An artist's retreat, it looks out on the Yarra Ranges; once the bush had been ablaze, but it has come back serenely; mist slowly rises out of a rich green blanket of new, young vegetation; it must have missed those fires by a whisker.

Ian has emerged after hearing our arrival. He is of rugged build – short and stocky. His eyes might be unseeing, but they appear to be alive to all that's around. He urges himself towards us, limping with the aid of a crutch. He knows every inch of these surroundings, takes his outstretched hand in mine, and I feel its commanding grip, his leathery skin and workman's hands.

'G'day.'

He repeats the greeting. 'G'day, and thanks for coming, good to meet you. Don't worry, the stick's only temporary,' he says dismissively, as if he is about to toss it.

'Accident. Charged off down the driveway without a passenger. Always need someone to steer. That's my wheels over there,' he says, gesturing in the exact direction where I am admiring a low-slung recumbent bike with large cycle wheels; sophisticated, beautiful.

Gyro Gearloose would have loved it.

'Designed it myself,' he says. 'But 10km on the roads around here is about all the exercise I get not being able to go out alone.'

'But that's enough of that,' he says, 'We'll be late for the pub,' and heads straight for David's car. I assume he placed it there from the sound of its arrival. But no: 'I can see shapes,' he says, climbing into the front seat.

The pub: a single poker machine is in operation, it's the local RSL. David finds a quiet corner that's warmed by the sun. Ian's blind eyes seem to have sight of my face and are unnerving me.

I want to know what happened to the Lawthers' son.

'The judge praised Stephen,' he says suddenly. 'Praised him for his bravery in testifying.'

'He also told the priest's barrister he would never permit a witness to be maliciously grilled, the way that bastard had attacked my boy, in any court of his, ever again.'

'That lawyer had called our son a liar,' says Ian, with anger and disbelief. '*Liar!*' that bastard had screamed at Stephen.

'Our son was struggling to come to terms with his life when he had earlier been forced to front Pell's measly Melbourne Response.' (The Australian cardinal had priced each case of abuse at a maximum of $50,000, no matter the circumstances.)

'There's another bastard,' Ian says.

David and I agreed. 'You won't get any argument from us.'

Ian tells us they weren't to expect even as little as $50,000. 'That was before we stepped into the court,' he says.

Ian was told he wouldn't be welcome at that initial hearing, anyway. 'Steve was to attend the hearing unrepresented. He found himself on one side of a table with 4 or 5 expensive lawyers for the Church on the other side. Our son had to convince them first, or there'd be no further court action.'

'Pity I didn't get to hammer the priest who molested my boy.' It won't be the first time I will hear Ian express that regret.

His voice fades, before summoning up a new thought from deep in his soul, and he speaks of the day he faced that miserable Pell group himself.

'"You're no more than a secondary victim in this," they said to me.'

'And that from a Church that is happy to fill the coffers of the legal profession, focusing on its own preservation. Not its crimes.'

<>

'You know there are some "good-uns" among the priests,' he says. 'Not that I've met too many lately. But they are still about.'

'Father Kevin Dillon is one. He was instrumental in setting up the survivors' network: "Lifeboat". In Geelong. 87 kilometres from Ballarat. And also one of Cardinal Pell's haunts.'

'Apart from Father Kevin, I have been cut off completely. The priest here now says Mass in the sister church 20 km away. Because of me. And my calling out. He says stuff about me in the newsletter, about me being a liar. Other stuff.'

'The Church of Pope Francis isn't about priests like him. More like Kevin Dillon. With his *Lifeboat*,' repeats Ian, and changes the tune. 'You go to church?'

The question is not a surprise, and I quickly answer: 'Yes. But I'm surprised that you would. After what you've been through. Helen and I have left the institution of the Catholic Church; we have our own community church. Still Catholic, God's mercy, justice, and equality. Grace. Most of us had been followers of an amazing Jesuit priest, Father Paul. Don't know where we'd be if it wasn't for this pope, though.'

Ian nods appreciatively. 'Guess you must have found a "good-un". The community I belong to now is all those the Church has hurt. We're all victims fighting for justice. Most, like Chrissie Foster, have given up on the Catholic Church.'

I gaze at him with such empathy it will have my brother and me locked into Ian Lawther's orbit until his tragic death – "at the hands of the Catholic Church", one can sadly say – on the 18th of August 2024.

Meanwhile, the mention of one of the bravest women on the planet is a reminder of *Hell on the Way to Heaven* by Chrissie Foster and Paul Kennedy, the horrific story of how two of the Fosters' daughters were raped by their parish priest at their local Catholic primary school.

David has arrived with the prescribed lunches. Ian says he has sworn off alcohol. Says he 'can't afford to trip up'. We'll drink water.

'How is your son?' I ask, finally.

'Being a dad. Stephen's wife got sick, and they were unable to save her, she died. Their daughter, Chloe, has become the focus of his life. She runs his life, is keen to check out every new girlfriend. She does like his latest, it appears. We live in hope. They're just up the road from us. Steve's been known to join me in the cart. He steers while I pedal,' Ian says with a rueful smile.

His mind seems far away, before he returns with a solemn face. 'Yes, we're both being dads now. Me with him and him with Chloe. But I'm still sorry I didn't get to hammer the priest who molested our son. And of course, with me being "a secondary victim" in the Church's eyes, I guess my wife is too. Pam has been a staunch Catholic. She took the abuses real bad.'

Ian tells us he had spent the previous day at a "Reclaiming Abuse Rally".

'There were over a hundred victims and their supporters outside the scene of Cardinal Pell's alleged crimes. St Patrick's Cathedral. Judy Courtin was there. She's an amazing advocate, has made a specialty of working in child sex abuse. I spent some time speaking with Chrissie. We're good friends. And Paul Kennedy.'

When he falls into an ominous silence, back there with his "community", I tell him I have read *Hell on the Way to Heaven*.

'It is a real wake-up for the Church,' he says.

'The law will catch up with people like Cardinal Pell,' he says, his voice gone soft but true.

'We're after him, we'll keep putting up that rainbow of ribbons on the Ballarat cathedral fence. Every time they take them down, we'll put more of them up. You know there have been 12 suicides, so far, many under the cardinal's watch,' he says and pauses before he speaks again.

'Cardinal Pell is no man of God.'

'You can't mention God, not among those survivors,' he adds quietly. 'I don't know why they blame God. Or Jesus. When it is the Church. But they don't see it. They can't. I've been tossed out of so many victim's homes, just for mentioning God,' Ian says.

<>

We have returned to Ian's home, the house in the trees.

'Out of mud and sticks in the sticks,' says Pam, who has been waiting eagerly for our return. 'Built it with our son, Adam.'

Pam is obviously proud of her man. 'But he couldn't have built it without Adam,' she says. 'Although Ian was near blind by then, our son needed his know-how.'

Ian Lawther was known by the locals as "the man who could do anything". 'But that is all in the past now,' Pam adds with certain sadness. 'But we love it here in this place.'

This place, at the foot of the Great Divide; an artist's mecca, with potters, painters, poets, writers and filmmakers for neighbours. It can't be bad.

But none are more talented, or more extraordinary than Ian Lawther, the brilliant craftsman and builder whose last job had been deemed impossible – until he solved it and made new friends for life.

We are about to see it.

<>

'Would one of you mind going into my study? You'll find a red, leather-bound album there. If you could bring it here, please?'

Ian has livened up after the habitual cup of tea. 'I want you to see something of what I used to be good at.'

I choose to be the bearer and find myself cradling a piece of history with gold-embossing on the cover: "THANKS," it says in very large letters, and beneath it: "For Ian and Pam".

We are gazing at Ian's greatest work, exquisite wood panelling and heavy beams, lead-lined windows, and the much-used floorboards from the foot-traffic of many a yesteryear. 'It was a games room,' he reminds us, 'and library. 300 years old and once in a Scottish castle. My clients bought it, had it shipped to Australia. The only instructions I got was a photo the size of a postage stamp.'

The ancient artefact had arrived in three containers, thrown in there haphazardly, the pieces unnumbered. Countless times its new owners had been told to 'throw it on the fire'.

'It's useless to me in that condition,' one of seven prospective builders had apparently said before Ian Lawther, the patient craftsman, painstakingly put it back together and restored its former glory. With love.

We gaze forlornly at a giant of his industry, my brother and I, as we're told Ian Lawther has a permanent invitation to visit the ancient trophy room whenever he likes. He tells me the owners are away, but he has a standing invitation to bring people to see it. Even though he can't.

Yes, one day we would see it, we'd love to.

But this man of surprises has another in store.

'When you do come, I will take you to the Grampian Ranges.'

The Bible Museum: he says we will find 2,000 old bibles there, owned by one family, a husband and wife. It was their life's work. Apparently, Ian Lawther is a welcome visitor there, too.

'Mrs. Enid Reid. She says it is their pride and joy. She once let me hold her most prized, and ancient possession. It was massive, heavy. It was totally handmade. It was awesome – to have a four-hundred-year-old treasure in my hands like that.' He wished he could see it.

'Shakespeare's time!' he exclaims. 'I could take you there also, sometime,' he repeats, as a satisfied smile reveals itself on his time-worn, ravaged face.

The mood has changed, and I cheekily inform him it would be a long way from Healesville to the Grampian Mountains in his pedal cart.

'Just don't ask my *young* brother to steer,' David says.

'How old are you?' Ian asks me suspiciously.

'It's David's little trick. There's ten years between us. You can figure that out.'

'You have to be 70?'

'Keep going. Way past 70. I liked your Bible story. It isn't about church, is it? Faith? I guess the personage we call God is in all of us,' I say, having latched on to something Ian had said earlier.

He reminds us right on cue. 'Don't forget there's some "good-uns" among the priests,' he says. We know he means it.

He slides a manila folder into my hands.

Strangely comforted by the irony, I turn to my brother, share his wry but disbelieving smile. I know it won't be the last time I will speak with this courageous man who had once sought retribution and to punish a priest – with his own bare hands.

Although he has every reason not to, this amazing man of true faith will tell me he is hanging onto hope in the Church of Pope Francis (I will tell him the church I frequent believes the South American is our only hope).

I open the folder he has given me, and begin to read what unfolds, aloud. Put together from the transcript of Ian's time before the Royal Commission, Ian's recounting of that time begins with a plea.

<><>

2014
The Transcript

'My name is Ian Lawther,' he says, announcing himself to the Royal Commission into Institutional Responses to Child Sexual Abuse. Ian is respectful, hopeful and begins nervously.

'Please hear my story. I am severely vision-impaired with no sight in my left eye and only four per cent sight in a restricted peripheral in my right.

'This blindness came about because I was looking at my daughter's baptismal certificate one day and I realised that a short time before the baptism, this same priest had sexually abused my son. I got so angry that I flew into a murderous rage, resulting in a burst blood vessel in my left eye. Later, I developed a tumour on my pituitary gland. The resulting operation to remove it damaged the optic nerve, resulting in trouble in my right eye.'

'Even after payment of compensation, which is kept to a minimum anyway, a person can be pulled back into the abuse mode by any one of a thousand triggers – going past a church, seeing a hierarch act as though he has a right to lead and, in such a superior manner, proclaiming the Church's innocence and screaming like a bully who has been caught out but knows there is worse to come.'

The Commission fell into a reverential hush as Ian Lawther recounted all that had taken place in the Catholic Church's efforts to deny his family justice.

He referred to his current local priest who had protested at Lawther's attack upon the Church. Why? 'He said there had been *"only two paedophile priests* in the parish's recent times". Can you believe anyone would say that?'

He described being silenced when he attempted to tell his story to his church's congregation.

'After which the priest moved the Mass away, where he had a letter read out in the new church naming me as his reason to do this.'

'The way that church service was stacked to shut up anyone the priest chose to was absolutely gutless and unfair to a person who was trying to speak for the children and shows just another way the Catholic Church is willing to lower itself to hold onto power.'

Ian Lawther informed the Commission he had 'followed protocol' and delivered a letter of complaint to Canberra, where the Vatican's diplomatic representative, the Papal Nuncio, resides. He had revealed himself as Australian, had titled his heart-felt missive "A Fair Dinkum Letter to the Pope" and hadn't received a reply.

'The Nuncio told me my letter* is probably buried in the Vatican complaints office, where he said there is a special file marked "Never to be answered".'

'At least he was honest,' Ian tells me of the only official from the Catholic Church who showed him some empathy. Ian's letter to the pope represents a major betrayal of a once-devout church goer.

'My working life was cut short,' Ian Lawther informed the hushed Commission, 'and I was forced on welfare 15 years ahead of my time.'

Ian's letter is included in the Appendices, with the family's permission.

<><>

2021
Silenced in Lismore

'Please call Del McBee,' Ian had said. 'You'll find her story devastating, hard to believe.'

This coming from a father of an abused son who had experienced the worst the Catholic Church could throw at anyone; I am in deep trepidation as I dial the number.

Ian has got there before me to make sure it is picked up; the phone is answered instantly, and soon I will be hanging onto every word.

Del McBee says she is 73 and tells me her story over a 43-minute phone call in which she barely draws breath, her anger is so palpable.

The decades of living with the trauma haven't dimmed her memory of being raped repeatedly by a priest everyone loved, as a little girl who, 60 years ago, he had made his own.

'I've been recently punched in the guts again,' she says, her words loud with "effs" and "cees".

Dell describes the Northern Rivers of NSW as 'the third worst area for child sexual assault in the Catholic Church'.

She says it is one that has gone under the radar, swamped only by the horrors found in Cardinal Pell's early domain, Ballarat. 'They're continuing to stalk that cunt, and I hope someone necks him.'

After a pause, the angry woman on the other end of the phone tells me: 'I finally got that lowlife bastard.'

'Rex Brown, *Father* Rex Brown,' she says with mind-numbing derision. Like all these cunts, it was decades before they got him.'

'Took the Royal Commission to get him,' she says, after a coughing fit. 'Took 50 years – of my life! Can you imagine that? – for them to put him in jail.'

'Course, they could've given the cunt 40 years but at his age, he was only ever going to last ten. He's dead now, just died, I hope he's in Hell. But what would that achieve? Anyone who has been through what I have will know what Hell is, and if I could still pray, I would be hoping that dead, he's getting it worse.'

Del McBee is a shadow of her former self. She tells me she is broken: 'I'm broken spiritually, scared to go out of the house.' Says she only makes short trips, and mostly to get food.

'But I'm writing. Gotten ten pages in. Want people who haven't been there to know. Those still in the Church. Especially those in the Church. Oblivious. Putting stories like mine behind them every day.'

She says: 'I went to the police one time, (and) a young female constable took me into a room to get my story down. But I had to break off, with my shaking, (I asked) could I come back tomorrow and finish that testimony? She said yes. And when I got there the next day, I was told the young constable had resigned, they said she had been only "probationary, she'd made a mistake joining the police".'

'The superintendent appeared sympathetic, until I asked for my testimony back. Bastard said they had been through all her papers, and there was no such testimony there.'

'The cunts had thrown it out, along with her.'

<>

After a pause, in which I assume the distraught woman has collected herself, the story of Del McBee takes another turn, when she speaks of "the others": Del's empathy for victims of priests has, she says, drawn her out in support of them all.

'As it does – when you're looking for someone to share what you have been through.'

'Others like me were going to the police at that time. Here's one story that'll knock you right out.'

I am being told in a few words: 'One day, there was a hit and run, the woman was killed. "We" – that group of us fucked off with the Church – we knew, because she had told us, she'd been on her way to the police station. To tell her story and get justice. But she got death.'

'And – you will not believe me when I tell you that woman was run over by a police car! *She was a victim twice over,*' she shouts from the rooftops.

And when she calms down, she says: 'You can put all that in your book, if you like.'

I say I will. 'I promise.' I tell her I will not change a word.

'You just keep on writing,' I say, feeding into the psychology of "getting it out". 'There must be more to your story.'

<>

There is, and in a calmer moment, Del tells me she is one of ten children, her family steeped in religion, her grandfather's potato farm all over the Dorrigo Plateau where, despite giving up on Church authority, sometime in the distant past he nevertheless built the first church in the district.

'Built it himself.'

Del McBee describes herself to me as 'a struggler from out bush' who, 60 years ago, was raped continually by her local priest, and has been fighting the Catholic Church ever since. Yet, Del still finds time to talk to me about her town's pain after it was ravaged by the floods and fires of climate change.

Six decades on from the terrible molestation by a priest Del once trusted, she knows her story is, to the Catholic Church, just a number in a Vatican file (declared to be upwards of 6,000, according to a priest I knew who spent three years in the Vatican).

And while even the crimes of the *Cosa Nostra* are openly displayed in the famous *Mafia Museum* high in the lonely hills of the tiny Sicilian town of Corleone – where I once saw walls of thick red cardboard folders on display for all to peruse – the Catholic Church is without a conscience – the files that contain its horrors languish in a Vatican file: "Never to be opened".

<><>

2017
Contrition

'I was devastated after the assaults, every one of them.'

'So distressed would I become that I would attend confessions weekly.'

'Talking about it was like a magic wand had been waved over me.'

'Confession gave me solace.'

'On every occasion, I was told by the fellow priest I spoke with to "go home and pray".'

Father Michael McArdle, addressing a Queensland court, after he had provided an affidavit, in which he said he had 'confessed 1,500 times to 30 different priests over a 25-year period'.

The judge put the marauding priest away – for six years. McArdle had faced 62 counts of abusing 14 boys and two girls over the previous two decades.

Michael McArdle resigned from the priesthood at the turn of the millennium.

During his time as a priest, he had sought the only refuge available to him to "save his soul" – the secrecy of the confessional.

He had made every priest he encountered complicit in his crime.

While every one of his victims had experienced Hell.

On Earth.

Where Christians pray, "God's will be done on Earth as it is in Heaven".

<>

Here's a marauding man of the cloth who has proved to be not so contrite: currently in jail – since 1994 – for the sexual abuse of over 70 children. August 2024 saw Father Gerald Ridsdale, (then) aged 90, convicted of eight more offences of raping children.

The closest Gerald Ridsdale had come to admitting remorse was when he said he blamed the Catholic Church for failing to stop the abuse he committed.

Ridsdale told a court that the Church had known – even before his ordination – that he had "a problem".

Sent for occasional counselling, the serial child rapist enjoyed the protection given him by loose-thinking bishops with no sense of what's right.

Hierarchs such as the Bishop Ronald Mulkearns and Cardinal George Pell, who didn't report Father Gerald Ridsdale to the police.

<><>

2002
Lucky to be a Cardinal

But unlucky to be a child in the Catholic Church.

'We all knew that Jack fooled around with little boys,' a priest once confided to the Investigative Unit at the *Boston Globe*.

'Priests told us they thought they maintained their celibacy vows if they molested boys and not girls,' reported the newspaper's investigative unit, *Spotlight*.

Two decades have passed since the acclaimed American newspaper began publishing stories of abuse within the Boston diocese, accusing 249 priests: their victims totalling over 1,000.

Those stories came to number 600.

'As a kid I was an altar boy,' *Globe* Editor Walter Robinson told the *New Yorker* issue of December 2015. 'Now I look back and I feel blessed. I thank God no one ever laid a hand on me.'

Author of its cover story, "Spotlight and its Revelations", Sarah Larson reports that Bernard Law – the first hierarch of his standing to be recalled to Rome for concealing priests' crimes – was "punished" by being reassigned by the Vatican to a plum position at Rome's Basilica de Santa Maria Maggiore, one of the highest-ranking churches in the Catholic world.

Lucky to be a cardinal – but unlucky for their victims!

The Boston research had uncovered the unsurprising news that 50% of the city's male clerics were sexually active.

While such a figure is almost certainly conservative, there's also the staggering revelation that one in ten was a paedophile.

The revelations in the 2015 Academy Award-winning film *Spotlight* continue to see audiences frozen to their seats in awe of its chilling message: that molesting priests had been active in over 45 American cities.

Apart from Boston, where the sexual abuse of children by Catholic priests had raged unabated while protected by the paradoxically-named Cardinal Law, the roll-up of clerical crimes cuts a vast swathe across the length and breadth of the United States, and includes Albany, Altona, Anchorage, Baker, Baltimore, Billings, Bridgeport, Burlington, Camden, Lake Girardeau, Charleston, Cincinnati, Cleveland, Dallas, Denver, Detroit, El Paso, Fort Worth, Grand Rapids, Indianapolis, Kansas City, Los Angeles, Memphis, Nashville, New York, Philadelphia, Phoenix, Pittsburgh, Rochester, Seattle, Toledo and Washington.

"Major abuse scandals have been uncovered all over the world", proclaimed *Spotlight*, naming countries as far-flung from each other as Argentina, Australia, Austria, Brazil, Canada, Chile, England, France, Ireland, Mexico, New Zealand, Nigeria, Peru, Scotland, South Africa, Spain, The Philippines and Venezuela.

Australia was not immune from the worst atrocities; our major cities and rural enclaves had fallen victim repeatedly. But none evoked more despair than the "city of gold", Ballarat, where newspaper reports claimed 26 had died by their own hand. (The Royal Commission saw a survivor hold up a photo of his class of 33 young boys. "12 had suicided," he said).

<>

'If the crimes of the priests were mentioned (amongst the thousands of pages the *Boston Globe* managed to obtain by court order) they were often referred to as "sins", for which the priest had repented and been forgiven,' Walter Robinson told the legendary New Yorker, its feature story as ground-breaking as the *Globe's*; its authors believing sin is the key to the Vatican's understanding of child rape.

They think it is an otherwise "innocent outlet", the view designed to avoid the criminal justice system.

'Does the Church get it?' asks the *New Yorker's* crack investigative journalist Sacha Pfeiffer. 'Does it get how it totally affects you for the rest of your life?'

After the *Spotlight* revelations, the Americans were driven to reveal the full story.

The United States Conference of Catholic Bishops revealed that in a 50-year period, 4,390 priests were alleged to have abused 10,667 of America's children. August 2016 saw one State alone release a grand jury report stating that since 1948 there had been 1,000 incidents of sexual abuse against children in that State by 300 priests.

But, with the statute of limitations of the Church in Pennsylvania cutting off victims' rights to apply for compensation up to age 30, and others, such as Alabama and New York placing the age at 21 and 23, even those low numbers didn't deter the Catholic Church from spending $4.5 million on employing "experts" to lobby their State legislatures for protection against being sued.

Pennsylvania State representative Mark Rozzi says he was raped by a priest when he was 13 but when he presented a bill to raise the statute of limitations, the Church 'hired 39 lobbyists to lobby 50 senators.'

'People are fed up with hypocrisy. Either you're protecting your bank account or you're protecting kids who got abused. It's not a tough choice. It's all about money.'

Surely the decision was simple, continues Rozzi: 'The Church with all their lobbyists and law firms… Or people like us?'

<>

It was a day for beginnings; but the first day of the Australian spring of 2016 in the Southern Hemisphere had already passed when two brave newspaper editors, one American, the other Australian, sat down for a chat in the latter's office at the feisty truth-seeking newspaper, the *Newcastle Herald.*

Chad Stone, the Australian, and the (now retired) editor of the *Globe*, Walter Robinson, are remarkable in that they had backed their reporters despite everything that was being thrown at them, as both papers relentlessly strove to tell the terrible truth that will change the Catholic Church forever.

'300 victims came forward in the first week (of the *Globe* breaking the story),' said Walter Robinson.

'Half of them were speaking out for the first time. On one occasion, the *Boston Globe* had to go to court to have a priest's file opened. The priest had sealed it – *never to be revealed,*'

Chad Stone reported that his award-winning ace reporter had joined her American counterpart when she matched the number of sex crimes by priests against children at 1,000 stories; the paper had also gone on to share her findings with the police.

'Here in Australia, Joanne McCarthy became part of the story,' Stone told Robinson.

The fiercely determined Australian journalist had been one of the first to declare there would be a Royal Commission into Institutional Responses into

Child Sexual Abuse.

'Because there must be,' McCarthy had said in her regular must-read column, *Shine the Light* – the aphorism headed up a campaign for justice – before going on to win the esteemed Walkley Award for quality journalism.

<><>

2017
A Terrible Paradox

Now it is a hot December day in Melbourne, and the Royal Commission is announcing its findings.

The long-awaited news won't give solace to a Church in peril; one that has so far failed to truly examine its conscience, its very heart, on its greatest crisis since the Reformation and French Revolution.

And a crisis it is fighting to survive.

<>

"The future belongs to those who see it coming," said David Bowie, à la *Ziggy Stardust*, and when the Royal Commission homed in on *Confession* and *Celibacy,* it has become apparent there's only one way forward for a Church in peril.

Many of us have been ready for the Vatican to see common sense. To see its errors, the fundamentals that, while central to the Catholic Church, have brought it down.

The Church has failed us. Failed our children with its secrecy. The giant millenniums-old cover-up that denies justice to the thousands of victims of clerical crimes. It has been there all along. We saw it at its worst in the torturous story of Father McArdle's seeking absolution from 30 other priests.

Confession.

"The law of the land (must) *take precedence over the Seal of Confession"*, the Commission demands of the Catholic Church.

Secondly, the Church in Australia is asked *"to request the Holy See to consider voluntary celibacy for diocesan clergy".*

Many of us are already cheering.

Considering where the Catholic Church has been.

And where we have arrived.

Catholics won't have long to wait for the Church's reaction from its out-of-touch men.

Men, the Church's centre of power in a world without women.

<>

The Church is in arrogant denial, with none of the Australian archbishops prepared to accede to the Commission's demands.

Cardinal Pell is in Rome, presumably scheming with his ultra-right friends to undermine Pope Francis's reforms, so it doesn't take rocket science to know where he stands.

Sydney's Anthony Fisher is a flashily out-of-touch medieval dresser who once admonished the Fosters to 'stop dwelling crankily on old wounds!'. A small-minded man who I once heard say he 'hates whingers', Fisher was at World Youth Day 2008, where he chided authority figures who take the stance.

Archbishop Dennis Hart is more subdued, saying: 'These matters must be referred to Rome.'

Melbourne's top cleric is used to passing on grave matters, having denied true justice to numerous victims under his watch. Hart by name but not by nature, he gave many a cruel reply to priests' victims, including Chrissie and Anthony Foster, who remain determined to keep on fighting for justice for all those let down by the Church's response to its true crimes.

But, of the three tall hats, the one reformists thought was in our corner, and at least reasonable, surprisingly turns out to also be a let-down.

Archbishop Mark Coleridge has, up to now, appeared to understand why the "people of God" are deserting the institutional Church, and what is at stake.

But he is speaking as Head of the Australian Bishops Conference, a job he wishes to keep, and his mealy-mouthed words give no hope:

'Lifting the confessional seal and enforcing mandatory reporting will do little to save young people,' is his reply to a rite that will be easily fixed by the law of the land.

And yet, Pope Francis needs all the help he can get from his bishops. To save the Church from itself.

We are seeing an untimely disaster.

One that is wrapped in words that surely must be heeded by the Vatican and, after its years of listening to horrific stories, one account of child abuse after another, the Commission is neither afraid to mention the word held sacred by Catholic traditionalists (in the face of reformists' pleas).

It is Catholicism's own revered "C" word, and the Church will hold onto it tooth and nail, despite the Vatican's occasional allowing of married Protestant converts to the Catholic priesthood, along with their wives.

Celibacy: the hypocrisy is finally on trial.

The Royal Commission couldn't have couched it in stronger words:

"Child sexual abuse is a canonical crime against the child (that must be seen not as) moral failings or as breaches of the 'special obligations' of clerics and religious to observe celibacy."

It brings the usual uproar from the out-of-touch faithful.

<>

I speak to a born-and-raised Catholic lawyer.

'Where's the evidence that obligatory celibacy has anything to do with sexual abuse?' he asks in measured tones, reminiscent of long-practised days spent in court.

Trapped in his traditionalist upbringing, he has long maintained his criticism of the Royal Commission. Thrown a blanket over his heart. But – now – have its findings changed his mind about the Church?

No.

'Not at all. There are five sacred rites that are unique to our faith, and confession and celibacy are the most important. The *very* most important,' he emphasises, with unsurprising tautology.

Change those, and 'we might as well be Protestants', he says with glaring contempt, and continues to add to my education.

'Celibacy hasn't been a problem for the Church since the 12th century when an ecclesiastical council was forced to deal with Catholicism's "inheritance" problem.'

'That's well known,' I say shortly. 'But...'

'But what?'

'Perhaps denying priests and nuns one of our most natural functions...' I look him in the eye. 'Where did that council say nuns and priests couldn't have sex? Surely consensual sex is God's plan? Take a look at it.'

And where does that get me? The lawyer is already walking away.

<>

'Celibacy? It's ridiculous!', historian Lord Norwich once told Phillip Adams on the *ABC's* iconic radio show, *Late Night Live.*

Declaring himself to be agnostic, John Julius Norwich's *The Popes* rips over a 2,000-year journey that focusses on saints and sinners, as well as unspeakable debauchers among the men of the early Church.

A favourite early pope of the canny writer is the 6th-century's Formosus, who was such a bad boy his successor had his bones dug up, the pope retried, his fingers hacked off and the rest of the poor sod tossed in the Tiber.

<>

'I'm as celibate as any priest,' says master of satire, the American author, Kurt Vonnegut, reflecting upon the impossibilities of steering clear of sexual intimacy.

He said it in his autobiography; wherein, published at the time of Trump, Vonnegut's *A Man Without a Country* contains hidden gems, including the best advertisement for Christianity I have ever read (on page 81 of my copy, published in 2005 by Seven Stories Press).

"If what he said is good, and so much of it is absolutely beautiful, what does it matter if he was God or not? But if Christ hadn't delivered the Sermon on the Mount, with its message of mercy and pity, I wouldn't want to be a human being. I'd rather be a rattlesnake."

<>

The snakes are apparently in the Vatican, where the Church appears practised at keeping secrets, and especially when they encompass crime.

In 2023, Chrissie Foster released a second book, in which the mother who has been fighting the Catholic Church for justice over its crimes against her daughters discusses *Canon Law* 489, that orders all Church hierarchs from the pope and cardinals to the bishops of dioceses to maintain secrecy files – such as the 6,000 files known to be held in the Vatican – that could hurt the Church.

Co-authored with Paul Kennedy, Still Standing is an exhaustive dossier and account of how the "suppression of truth…in matters of faith and morals… keeps the crime of paedophilia alive".

"Children are easily intimidated and silenced (but) to be a sexual assault victim of Catholic clergy is to know your own truth, the truth of your own experience."

The Royal Commission decreed that "children are to be believed". But is the

Catholic Church listening?

"Cardinal Pell protected his own interests and his Church's finances. He let children suffer. He destroyed lives," write the authors of *Still Standing*.

Why is the Catholic Church so frightened of the truth when it is the only way to the future?

Justice and fairness in Christ's image.

<>

Nelson Mandela saw it in his bravely mounted initiative, *The Truth and Reconciliation Commission*, the door to the new South Africa.

Italy saw it in its opening up of the truth about the *enemy within*, with no expense spared in the state's long-running *Maxi (Mafia) Trials*.

Holidaying in Sicily once, Helen and I had passed the monument to the judges who had been slain by a car bomb; we headed up a winding road before arriving at a sleepy mountain village, nestled high in the hills above Palermo. It would be easy to bypass Corleone; but our small group of "modern" Catholics was keen to see the "Mafia Files" that are housed in a purpose-built museum. A reminder of Jerusalem's Holocaust Museum, the walls of red folders, detail the court records of *Cosa Nostra* criminals, and their message: "Never Forget".

I found myself in awe that day of the Italian State's determination to find justice and was screaming inside: *'Open those Vatican Files – Pope Francis!'*

You are the Church's "godfather". Open the incriminating files. Truth-telling is the way to the future.

Reform starts with the Church coming clean about its crimes.

Open every file. Climb that mountain of hidden stories locked away in the hope they will all be forgotten.

Sadly, the Catholic Church is so often spoken in the same breath as the Mafia; the Church's crimes against humanity are staring us in the face – the betrayal of those Pope Francis calls empathetically, the "little ones".

<><>

2016
Another Very Brave Man

And so it goes.

In a continuum of horrors for the Catholic Church, the massive list of child sex molestations is echoing to the sound of thousands of feet, departing the pews.

Every such crime perpetrated upon a child is different; but every one of those horrors has something to say about Church inaction.

Some victims don't hold back on the graphic detail; what happened to them rivals accounts from the Jewish holocaust.

And James Miller's story illustrates the evils of Catholic Church inaction at its worst.

The writer of a tell-all book, *The Priests,* Miller describes being consistently raped as a child by men of the cloth who had won his trust. Who controlled him. Twisted him to their evil will – and for anyone left doubting *what child rape is,* read James' story.

Openly honest as the day is long, it belongs on the cross of Jesus.

The Vatican has the moral obligation to address the evil that is destroying the Church.

To do so is as simple as breathing: like all matters of morality and of the justice Christianity faces, it begins with the question:

What would Jesus do?

What does God expect of us in the face of the evil in our midst as honestly portrayed by very brave victims of child sexual abuse – such as James Miller in *The Priests*?

<>

"To be forcefully sexually penetrated against your will is all violence and shock," Miller writes.

"Everything else that (his school's headmaster) Father Thomas Brennan (no relation to the respected Jesuit intellectual, Frank) had done to me – the sexual touching, masturbation, forced kissing – even though it had driven me to the point of being physically sick, seemed mild in comparison."

"In the violation of penetrating abuse, you try not to look or think about what is happening. This you do with great determination."

"I developed a habit that I follow to this day – I never go anywhere without something to read."

"I did this to counteract the obsessive thinking about him."

"I felt disgusted, dirty beyond redemption, shocked. I felt small and of less consequence.

"This must stay between us, James."

"This is normal between men," the young boy was told by his abusive priest.

"He took pleasure from it," Miller says, "It was pure indulgence in which I was a mere object."

"Everything about the priest's attitude said he believed he was entitled to behave as he did."

And when young James complained? "We won't put up with boys telling lies about Father, or anyone else," he was told by the one person he went to for help, another abusive priest. Miller has had to wait 30 years to see justice for himself and the priest who had serially raped him brought to trial.

He writes in his book about an earlier judgement that had brought him, and the others that Father Thomas Brennan had sodomised, small solace, when Brennan, escaping true justice himself, was only convicted for "concealing the crimes of a fellow priest – his friend, John Sydney Denham".

Father Denham was found to have escaped the law for two decades during which he molested 57 boys. He was sentenced to 19 years' incarceration.

James Miller's memoir describes a schoolfriend unwittingly complaining about Denham to the abusive Brennan.

"Get out of here with your fantasy stories," he was told.

Sadly – for Miller and the others Brennan had molested – their abuser died before he could be sentenced.

Father Thomas Brennan was a criminal lauded by the Church, having once been given the status of Vicar-General, a role that gave him the powers vested in a bishop (including, it seemed, to do as he willed with young boys).

<>

Meanwhile, James Miller went on to become a successful lawyer; but his life was spiralling out of control; he was in grave danger.

Joanne McCarthy, the award-winning journalist and author of over 1,000 stories about the institutional child sexual abuse crisis in her neck of the woods to Sydney's north, was a privileged confidante.

"It was 1997," she writes, "He was drunk. He'd made the decision to end his life in an entirely matter-of-fact way after his (equally) inebriated barrister mate lurched away to find a toilet. James Miller stepped out onto the window ledge… he was 35."

The way James tells it, if it wasn't for his friend being a big man and with the strength to hurl him back from that parapet four-stories up, he would have been another suicide among the many in the terrifying litany of Catholicism's lengthening list of crimes.

Instead, he has become one of its major adversaries, determined to seek recompense from the Church that so comprehensively failed him.

Joanne McCarthy describes the boy, James Miller/

"He was a popular teenager, a blonde-haired, blue-eyed surfer in a town where his type were gods."

He was destined "for great things".

The Priests charts a torrid journey in which Miller marries and becomes a lawyer until, unable to reconcile with his past, his life unravels, he drinks to forget, only to begin a life on the streets, lost and bewildered.

He says in the book: "I knew my abnormal psychology was moving towards a kill-or-be-killed proposition; either I deal with it; or it could take me out."

"I'm going to fight and I'm going to win," he writes, determined to take on the Church (in a civil action) and its celibacy rule that he believes is responsible for the horrors he experienced as an altar boy at the hands of a monster, masquerading as a priest.

"The battleground is the Catholic Church and celibacy," Joanne McCarthy agrees.

"The sexual abuse of our kids has been a crime in Australia for the past 150 years."

"In 1857, a John Kelly was put to death for the sodomising of a small boy and nine abusers have been hanged for it since," says McCarthy, who had initially been driven to expose the litany of serial sex abuse that had remained concealed in Newcastle and its environs, 160 kilometres north of Sydney.

"You had both the Catholic Church and (also) the Anglican Church with a succession of bishops making it pretty obvious that if you were a sex offender, 'you'll be safe up here.'"

<><><>

Three
SEE NO EVIL

2016
Caught in the Net

'Abortion is a worse moral scandal than priests abusing young people.'

George Pell said that to a 100,000-strong audience at Canada's World Youth Day in 2002, and in equal infamy, the same year had seen the *Boston Globe* begin publishing the results of an investigation that had revealed dozens of priests had found fodder prowling the youth of the "City on the Hill" for years.

The findings had claimed Pell's compatriot-in-crime, Boston Cardinal Benjamin Law. The hierarch's resignation was accepted by then Pope John Paul II.

The newspaper's specialised Investigative Unit would go on to give its name to the Oscar-winning film, *Spotlight.*

Law proved to be cut from the same arrogant cloth as Pell, when he hid behind the Vatican "veil", declaring 'the particular circumstances at this time suggest a quiet departure'.

While the priest-protector was quick to get to safety in Rome, thousands around the world were horrified by Law's parting words.

'Please keep me in your prayers.'

Although he was quick to add, 'pray for the victims – please!'.

Cardinal Law is the first of his kind to be caught up in the giant cover-up that has brought the Catholic Church to its knees.

Law would go on to live for another 15 years, yet another of the Vatican's most protected species.

He would die in his sleep, at the same age as the paedophile priest who had raped two of Chrissie and Anthony Foster's beautiful daughters: Father Kevin O'Donnell at 87.

O'Donnell was lauded over by his arch-protector in Australian Catholicism's highest office, Cardinal George Pell.

<>

In 2016, Pell reaches the age a cardinal was once obliged to retire, 75. (The decree was relaxed when Pope Benedict XVI returned the choice to the incumbent).

Many wish the controversial Australian will retire – for the sake of the Church. George Pell is the third-ranked hierarch after the pope; he is a hater of the pope's reforms but, with the ball in his court, insiders are telegraphing that the chance of a Pell retirement happening is, well, none.

But he is facing a new predicament that may lay a foundation to accelerate another cardinal's moving out of office.

<>

George Pell has been summoned to appear before the Royal Commission into Institutional Responses to Child Sexual Abuse.

Ever the wily escape-artist, Pell seems determined to remain in the relative safety of his home in Rome, claiming he is 'too ill to travel'.

Cardinal Pell is to be questioned about what he knew of the horrific crimes that had happened on his watch.

While Pell's non-appearance in his home country is a minor inconvenience to his determined inquisitors, he will be interviewed via video link from Sydney, where victims and their supporters will soon assemble both inside and outside the court in silent solidarity with those who are already in Rome.

Media contingents from around the world are already on their way to Rome, as is a small group of interested Australians, organised by James Miller, the determined lawyer. Anthony and Chrissie Foster, who have also found residence near the Vatican.

Some of the Australian press is doubting of Cardinal Pell's veracity with every demanding headline:

"SEE NO EVIL, HEAR NO EVIL, STOP NO EVIL" fills the front page of George Pell's hometown newspaper, the *Herald Sun*, while *The Sydney Morning Herald* is demanding Pell "SPEAK NO EVIL".

<>

Meanwhile, Pell is nonplussed at what he sees as a 'minor interruption' and he has his supporters, many with deep pockets, who will be happy to feed the man who wanted to be pope.

But George Pell doesn't fear anyone, he is politically savvy, and conscious of his powerbase in the Church and in the Vatican.

Only this time, he has met an especially formidable inquisitor: the irrepressible Gail Furness, who has been Counsel Assisting the Commission these past four years. Amazingly calm and knowledgeable, it appears the quietly spoken lawyer has assembled a dossier that would fill a library. She knows the Cardinal is a vast repository of knowledge about what has taken place in the Victorian Church, beginning with Pell's old stamping ground – Ballarat.

Ballarat has the terrible distinction of being Australia's worst Catholic diocese for clerical crimes. With so many suicides – as we have learnt, the numbers are 26 – it is not surprising that Chrissie Foster would write that during those times, in Ballarat "the most dangerous place for a child was a Catholic Church" (*Still Standing*, 2023).

Pell spent his seminarian years at Ballarat's ill-famed St Patrick's College and has returned in many official capacities since.

"The city of gold" could well be described as George Pell's "home".

Now he is in Rome, facing questions the Royal Commission wants answered.

Pell has told the media he sees what he calls an "Inquisition" as nothing but a flea on his back – or in his words, 'a minor irritation'.

But we can guess that it is to be seen for what it is, over the coming four days.

<><>

2016
"They use their tongues to deceive."
ROMANS 3:13

February. It's going to be a hot day at Smokey Cape Lighthouse where Helen and I have come for the isolation we both crave; to get away from the hurly-burly, it's perfect for a recharge. Friends will join us later today, and the setting of the sun will see a lone light nightly sweep the blackness of sea; we'll be in the comfort of the newly refurbished keepers' cottages by then.

There's no better place to catch the stars in the minutes between light-ups, while we drink to life and the rebirth of the Catholic Church, which is showing such promise under the guidance of the singular Argentinian who has offered hope of reform on his ascension to Peter's throne (or is it Paul's seat, Tarsus' favourite son, more in the likeness of Jesus' plan for loving communities than the politically-minded Peter, in preference to the Church-as-institution that was fashioned bureaucratically in the dictatorial way of the Romans – with the pope's infallibility, and all that? Lately, many of us reformists have been thinking so).

While the word is Pell and his righteous cronies – the hard men he leads – continue to work against the Francis reforms, the man who would be pope himself is to face interrogation from the Royal Commission about his role in the sexual abuse of children in Ballarat and other places, including (presciently) Melbourne's St Patrick's Cathedral.

The proceedings will be televised from Rome over the next four mornings from 5.30am, and I am not going to miss a second. I expect to see another chapter of this book open in front of my eyes.

I hope also to find some answers to the long, busy road of cover-ups that had its start for me over two decades ago; one day, I will face the Marist leader who was once my friend. After following him all the days he appeared at the

Commission, I have only one question left: *what the fuck was he thinking? When you got me involved in the worst crimes imaginable?*

'It's only *kiddy-fiddling*,' you said. 'The kids will get over it.'

What has the Marist leader been doing with his life since that dark day all those years ago? When any innocence I had left was compromised forever?

Atoning, I expect, on his knees every day, praying, hoping? As "defender and protector" where his chosen identity lies?

Learning where you went wrong?

I'm hearing priests say: 'I left the seminary knowing nothing about sex.'

And that's the truth of it – it was burned into me on that fateful day. When it was just you and me, and a secret ever since I have had to keep. When you failed to heed my advice: 'You must go to the police,' I had said to you then. 'You were Provincial of the Marist family; of over 2,000 of your Brothers across the South Pacific.'

You said: 'I can't do that.'

Despite the terrible crimes – of 'at least 150' you told the Commission.

'We could lose everything,' you told me, and we both knew it would be your word against mine.

'Some children can be provocative,' you had told me.

So, I was left with no option – as many other would-be whistleblowers also discovered: what was between us became a secret I was forced to keep – I knew you would deny everything for the sake of the damn Church – the *damned* Catholic Church – that, as an institution, is destroying itself.

I was forced to remain silent – for over 23 years! Until you were outed in the Royal Commission – where you met your match – as George Pell is about to discover – in the irrepressible Gail Furness, who once had you on toast, as she slowly drew out what you knew.

<>

Two years have passed since the Marist leader's appearance at the Commission freed me to tell the truth; and I have been hard at it ever since, writing it all down, what I know, what I have found out, and more.

Will he join me – wherever he is – in watching Cardinal Pell take his turn to face the music?

And hopefully, for the sake of thousands of children – Francis' "little ones" – be brought down.

Now that journey has taken me to a cardinal who, it seems, has more questions to answer than you can poke a mace at.

It is not looking good for Pell: his desire to protect the Church putting the price of the rape of a child at a maximum of just $50,000 is already unconscionable.

A paltry figure it is and yet the truth is, with most cases hard-fought by the Catholic Church, the average compensation currently stands at a measly $17,000; even then payouts are to be accompanied by a confidentiality clause that conveniently covers up the Church's betrayal. *Broken Rites.*

Some, such as the Fosters, weren't going to take that lying down, having led the charge against Pell's inspired meanness. Along with legal costs being awarded by the Victorian court in the family's favour, in 2013 Chrissie and Anthony Foster used their right to privilege at the Parliamentary Inquiry when they broke the confidentiality clause and announced they had been awarded $750,000.

'We defied the (Pell) ruling in the hope that others will also seek appropriate compensation from the Catholic Church,' Chrissie would say later.

But nothing will erase the evils done to their beautiful daughters by the shrewd child groomer they had once respected as a priest.

Father Kevin O'Donnell's career as a serial paedophile remains at the pinnacle of Cardinal George Pell's cover-ups.

Protected, one of the Catholic Church's most notorious criminals, is just another priest held in the Church's satanic bosom.

<>

The first day of the Rome hearings sees me rise at dawn. The proceedings haven't begun yet and, alone in this high place, accompanied by shrieks from the feathered "neighbours" whirling above, and sand and sea way below stretching far into the distance, I am a pilgrim once more, remembering the time Helen and I climbed Mt Nebo. We surveyed a different landscape then, it was all stones and dying trees; it didn't display much of the promise Moses saw when he accepted God's Commandments, grateful perhaps his people had been freed. Moses accepted all ten tablets then, and the values on them became the foundation platform of the three great religions much of the world acknowledges today.

But I am drifting away from the story about to unfold before my eyes on the small square "telly," which, though it is very small, will take up all my concentration for one-and-a-half hours from the get-go and over each of the next four days.

The proceedings will be televised on most Australian channels. I have chosen the national broadcaster, and at precisely 5.30am, the first of the four Pell hearing days begin.

There's no mucking around with introductions, and when the switch to Rome happens there's George Pell, holding back his arrogance and the impatience he is known for, his face impassive.

Determined to be in control of the situation he has found himself in, he will give nothing away that would feed into the secular law. His friend, the former Prime Minister Tony Abbott will later describe these proceedings as a "New Inquisition", but that is for later, when Abbott, who trained briefly to become a priest and had a Boxing Blue from Oxford, will join George Pell on the climate-denying trail, and more, both comfortable naysayers from the political right.

<>

A familiar face: we have come to know the steely-eyed Gail Furness. She is long-practised in such proceedings, and in the four years as Counsel Assisting the Commission, she takes no prisoners in seeking the truth.

<>

'It's a sad story and it wasn't of much interest to me. I had no reason to turn my mind to the extent of the evils that Ridsdale had perpetrated.'

Pell: speaking of the rampaging child molester, Father Gerald Ridsdale.

Furness is aware that George Pell has been aware of Ridsdale's offending since 1973. She knows that Pell escorted his friend to court once or twice (a factor that David Marr, writer of Pell biography *The Prince*, says may have swayed the judge to hand Ridsdale a more lenient sentence).

Pell makes a rare admission: 'The instinct was more to protect the institution, and the community of the Church, from shame,' he says.

'Really?' Furness is unimpressed. She has a big fish in her sights and aims to reel him in.

The *Broken Rites* repository of Catholic priests' crimes against children reports that Ridsdale had been abusing children ever since his ordination in 1961.

And "in the seminary before that" where he would have befriended a muscular ex-footy player, George Pell.

Despite being moved on 16 times, the fiend had gone on to rape "at least 65 children".

Among other reports, Ms Furness draws attention to a widely published 1993 photo of Pell escorting Ridsdale to court, after which the offender went on to face judgement seven more times.

'Many others must have known about his criminal activities,' states the Commission's Counsellor.

Pell tells Furness that he wasn't aware that 'Ridsdale's crimes had been common knowledge'.

The first time George Pell has described raping a child as a *crime* brings an intake of breath that can be felt all over the world.

Perhaps it is a first for the beleaguered Catholic Church.

<>

After the Ridsdale revelations and their implications for George Pell in the former's crimes, the next day in Rome sees that Cardinal Pell has readied himself to take the fight up to the Commission's Gail Furness.

Unused to being confronted by a woman, Pell will struggle with the questioning of such a calmly formidable foe – while battling to conceal his disdain.

I am also engaged in a battle with occasional signal loss: high in my mountain retreat, the others have removed themselves to the beach below where, lost in the shadows of the cliff, they are tiny stick figures; having left me to my fate.

Few of them are able to stomach such terrible truths: just give us the headlines later.

Later in the day, we will get the cards out, open bottles of wine and hope our trust in the Church of Pope Francis, with his focus on truth and mercy, will prove enough for us to keep the faith that has, up to now, held us precariously "in the palm of God's hand" (*Isaiah* 41:31).

<>

So: to another day, and first the cardinal is asked, in obvious disbelief, why he wasn't aware of what was going on when complaints were being constantly made by angry parishioners?

Pell stares down the Counsel Assisting and tells the steely-eyed Gail Furness:

'People complained in the Church all the time.'

'You were accepting of a priest's word?'

'If a priest was to deny such activity, I was strongly inclined to accept that denial.'

'Even if there had been many more accusations that pointed to child abuse activity?'

But it is Pell's next statement that will define him.

'Child sexual abuse has been a problem for society and the Church for centuries,' he says.

Clearly, the cardinal has been put offside by Furness' considerable abilities, her un-nerving appearance, and under her constant calm questioning, he will soon be battling to conceal his total disdain for the proceedings.

George Pell has withstood over four hours of relentless questioning and is in danger of losing his bottle. His interrogator is a woman, after all, and with women having no place – no power – in a Pell Church, it is no wonder.

<>

Meanwhile, Ms Furness is, in her customary way, as patient as a spider building a web.

The Counsellor is aware she has made her adversary uncomfortable in his own skin. After years diligently doing her unenviable job – Furness' patient probing of the Marist leader has proved to be a rehearsal – Furness utilises facts in measured sentences that are designed to unnerve, and will up the ante today with information that will rock the Catholic Church to its very foundations, as she fixes Pell with her unrelenting stare, and says from across the world.

"The Royal Commission has spoken to over 5,000 survivors, Cardinal."

Pausing.

'About their accounts of abuse, Cardinal Pell.'

'It is an astonishing number in anyone's estimation,' Furness tells him, and casually adjusts the lapel of her well-cut suit.

Every session has seen Gail Furness immaculately dressed in her customary pale colours, and today she has chosen grey tweed – an obvious favourite that suits her and is touched off by her habitual string-of-pearls necklace and matching earrings. Horn-rim spectacles complete her desired appearance; she is a learned species.

Pell's immediate adversary – there'll be others that will have him even less prepared – is a study of professionalism. Pell has met his match in Furness, who has been leading the Inquiry since its beginning, and the time of Pope Francis' ascension, in 2012.

She fixes her eyes sharply upon George Pell, and asks, 'Why had there been so many sexual abusers aggregating in Ballarat East in the 1970s?'

"You were there, Cardinal," she might have added, "You were in the thick of it, the Ballarat diocese infamous for its betrayal by priests that has resulted in multiple suicides so far, Cardinal Pell – you were there during those years, as a seminarian, priest, and also bishop."

But the Counsel didn't need to: Pell's frown continues his certain uneasiness and annoyance at the relentless questioning.

Stumbling over words that don't arrive easily, he casually admits it had been a 'disastrous coincidence', and in a manner highly uncharacteristic of his usually clear-mindedness, unused to having his views questioned, Pell finds he is forced to demean himself when he finds he is imploring the Commission to believe him.

'I had been deceived by others,' he says feebly.

They had 'kept information' from him.

Pell says he hopes the Counsel Assisting will accept his answer. 'Because I would have acted upon it,' he 'respectfully' hopes the learned Counsel accepts.

Furness has a word for Pell's answer.

'Implausible.'

The Counsellor says she doesn't believe him.

She adjusts her spectacles.

'I suggest, Cardinal, that the evidence you have given is designed to deflect blame from you.'

<>

The final session sees him, perhaps unsurprisingly, change tack when, ever the political animal who in the proceeding's intermission has spoken with the Catholic Church's lawyers, he grovelingly admits failure.

'The Church has made enormous mistakes and is working to remedy them,' he says.

But, of course, it is a lame excuse and is met with a stunned and doubting silence that doesn't get any better.

Cardinal Pell has failed in his quest to save the Church.

He has betrayed thousands of the youngest members of the Catholic faithful, their parents and minders.

He has mocked the facts, denied true justice to victims – and we have been told that the Commission has in its possession thousands of depositions accusing Catholic Church clerics of the molestation of children in its care.

Pope Francis' "little ones": those victims of the Church he leads – and has promised to support, with true justice.

We, the faithful, can only live in hope.

George Pell has captured the world's attention with the Catholic Church's failure in the crimes of a century; of the Church's greatest test since the Reformation and the French Revolution.

He has been accused of indifference to the terrible betrayal that took place in the Catholic Church's secret confines.

The actions of unempathetic men with deceitful tongues are reaching a crescendo.

But it can't be over for him yet; not by a long shot: Pell is on a slippery slope of his own doing and with questions mounting, truth will not be denied.

<>

Meanwhile, the small group of Australians who have been gathered near the Vatican, inside the Hotel Quirinale each day, eager for answers during Pell's grilling, live in hope that the world has been listening.

Victims and survivors of clerical abuse, they had travelled to the Rome hearing and are being mobbed by the hungry media. What has Pell's questioning achieved?

'Pell's appearance has gained us nothing.'

'He has been covering up the truth for years.'

'It all rests with Pope Francis.'

'I see no hope for the Catholic Church.'

Among them are those determined justice-seekers, Anthony and Chrissie Foster whose lives had changed when they learnt the monster housed in the presbytery of their local church had been abusing two of their daughters for years.

Blood on the Church's hands.

They will return to Australia, their hearts heavy with loss, and diminishing hope in the Church of Pope Francis.

But they will not give up their fight. Everything must start somewhere, and it is the memory of a meeting the Fosters once had with the hierarch at the top of his game – in the Vatican's eyes – who sits at the heart of the couple's fight to bring the Catholic Church to justice and bring about change.

<><>

1997
'She's Changed, Hasn't She?'

Chrissie and Anthony Foster had been asking to see Archbishop Pell for months. A year into his first high posting as Archbishop of Melbourne, the couple had sought an audience with the hierarch on their way home from Europe. Pell declined, but the Fosters persisted, and soon after, in February 1997, the meeting took place in Melbourne.

An ironic twist sees George Pell fresh from having allegedly molested two choir boys in the sacristy of Melbourne's St Patrick's Cathedral, and two decades hence will see the law's patience taxed as it chases the then cardinal across the world.

The Fosters' urgency had been stoked recently, when, in a move that can only be described as "evil", Pell had lauded over the funeral of Kevin O'Donnell, the priest who had abused the Fosters' children and countless others (a lawyer at the time referred to O'Donnell as 'a two-a-day' child molester).

Nonplussed by the visitors' determination to see him, Pell gave the couple 30 minutes, and it was towards the end that one of the most damning incidents in the history of Catholic child sexual abuse took place.

Chrissie: 'Anthony hastily produced the (incriminating) photos we had brought with us.'

They are of the same young girl, their daughter, Emma.

Here she is, gorgeous, happy, smiling; small, her teenage years are far off.

And here, in the second photograph?

Well, this one was taken some years later: gone is the happy young girl, her innocence stolen; her beauty struggles to shine through the razor cuts, the wounds on Emma's tearful face also weeping, the dark shades below her sad, vulnerable, haunted eyes…

…surely, they are – to a Catholic to his bootstraps – the *wounds of Christ – on the Cross!*

But – no – not to a man of near-ultimate power in the Catholic Church.

After chancing a brief look at the photographs before him, George Pell turns his eyes from them and dismisses what he has seen with a statement so self-damning I'm sure Chrissie had found it to be as difficult to write down, as I am now.

'She's changed, hasn't she?' he says and, swiftly turning on his heel, makes his exit from people he had made clear he hadn't wished to meet in the first place.

<>

She's changed?

I run the scene past my friend Nick; he has joined the throng of "leavers", most of whom, although Catholic by birth, have been angered and saddened by church inaction.

Nick's view is that 'People like Pell are a cruel, twisted manifestation of the Catholic Church's dark, hidden soul. Pell's lack of empathy is telling. He hasn't a moment for anyone, who isn't totally with him.'

But we will both carry the image of a photo – a photo we have only read about, haven't seen – forever and a day.

While that little girl had gone on to die a lonely death in her bedroom from a prescription drug overdose – Emma was 26 – her younger sister, Katie, had been trying to ease her pain with alcohol; later walking in front of a car, the resulting catastrophic injuries, mental and physical, requiring lifetime care.

Chrissie Foster continues to hold the Catholic Church to account and in 2019 will update *Hell on the Way to Heaven*, the book she wrote with the help of *ABC* journalist, Paul Kennedy, in the light of current findings.

Her story is both an important chronicle and an indictment of how the Catholic Church betrayed a once devout and loving family; and *Hell on the Way to Heaven* joins Boston film Spotlight in revealing a long catalogue of horrors the Catholic Church turned its blind eye to, as the ancient institution grew to be a *crime scene.*

Although the court awarded recompense of ten times the amount the

Catholic Church had been prepared to pay to victims, it will never make up for the hell on earth suffered by a Melbourne family who once saw regular visits to church as part of their life. However, the Fosters' bravery has paved the way for others to take on its fading institution and obtain the justice they deserve.

In 2018, then Victorian Premier, Daniel Andrews would drag the Church into sharing real compensation when he set aside $600 million for people who had been abused in institutions, all and sundry, as part of the Federal Government's National Redress Scheme.

Chrissie Foster sees little hope in the Catholic Church.

"My annihilated faith in the hierarchy of the Catholic Church meant that I had no confidence that they would do the right thing by treating children with respect and victims with generosity," Chrissie Foster writes in *Still Standing*.

I am privileged to have met Chrissie and I am grateful for the many discussions we have had, along with Ian Lawther, in the writing of *Betrayal*.

"Every rape of a child is horrific in its own way" – to borrow from Tolstoy's famous aphorism – but the stories of victims such as Ian, Emma and Katie Foster stand out as an indictment twice over of the Catholic Church.

<>

More brave souls are coming forward every day, and the Church of Pope Francis has fallen under siege.

As for George Pell, he and his allies in the Vatican will continue to attack the pope's reform agenda that, built in Jesus' true image of mercy and grace, is returning power to the people – *"the people of God".*

It is almost two millennia since the phrase was spoken by 2nd-century Catholic saint, Irenaeus, who had been asked where to situate the growing new religion's headquarters.

"The Church is where the people are," said the popular Bishop of Lyon, who has been described as "the Father of the Church".

<>

"The Church" – how easily the phrase slips off the tongue; but not so easily when the Catholic Church is so determined to consign its crimes to the dustbin of history.

Archbishop Fisher demanded Sydney audiences 'stop dwelling crankily on old wounds'.

Anthony Foster had seen the statement as a direct attack on his family. It was 'outrageous that Fisher had said it, but not unique in the Church,' Chrissie's equally strong-minded husband says.

Sadly, I found Fisher's statement was being unconscionably echoed by certain priests of the old Church, with one young Polish priest briefly of my acquaintance telling me one day over honey vodkas in a Warsaw Square: 'We should put the Church's current problems behind it and move on.'

Sadly, like Cassius, 'I thought I knew him well'.

<><>

2017
Goodbye, Brave Man

It's the 23rd of May, and Chrissie Foster's co-writer of *Hell on the Way to Heaven*, Paul Kennedy, interrupts the *ABC Breakfast* TV program he is co-hosting with the shattering news that Anthony Foster has passed away after a massive stroke.

Anthony Foster's final act of generosity will see a healthy liver successfully given to a teenage boy that very night. His kidneys will also give two dialysis patients new leases of life.

After which, that courageous fighter for justice, Anthony Foster, will be given a State funeral by the Victorian government that will "celebrate his grace and legacy in the fight against child sex abuse".

Kennedy will tell the thousands who had attended the funeral: 'Anthony Foster fundamentally changed Australia through his tireless campaigning to bring to account perpetrators (everywhere).'

Aimee, the Fosters' third daughter, will describe her father as 'pure of heart' and 'generous with his love, most of all, because this is where he knew real value (was)'.

Chrissie will later write in *Still Standing* of her husband's "fighting for justice for our daughters and all clergy victims".

Anthony Foster, a saint for our times.

Premier Daniel Andrews took the news of Anthony's funeral to the Victorian Parliament, and Chrissie Foster was declared Victoria's Local Hero in the Australian of the Year Awards.

'The very same title could have applied to her soulmate Anthony,' the Premier said.

'Because together they were heroes for justice, heroes for truth.'

<><>

2017
A Traitorous Pairing

Ever since Pope Francis' milestone meeting (known as a "synod", or meeting of the faithful) on the Catholic Church's approach to *Family* in 2015, the modern nature of marriage, tentative steps towards sensible birth control, divorce and same-sex couples – 'Who am I to judge?' says the pope of compassion and mercy – the Pell faction has been meeting regularly at the Cardinal's at Pell's personal creation – the money dragged from wealthy donors and the NSW Church – a hotel for pilgrims, *Domus Australia.*

Now, fresh from his tussle with the Commission and aware that politics and religion can be a potent cocktail when mixed, Pell and his co-conspirators have turned their dissatisfaction onto a current papal initiative, the saving of the planet; *Laudato Si'* – "Praise Be To You".

No previous papal letter has drawn as much attention as Francis' plea to save planet Earth from environmental destruction.

This is climate-change sceptic George Pell in his business suit, speaking in London in 2011 at a gathering of like-minded threats to the world, known as the *Global Warming Policy Forum.*

'Where does scientific striving become uneconomic, immoral, or ineffectual and so lapse into hubris?'

'Have scientists been co-opted on to a bigger, better advertised and more expensive bandwagon than the millennium bug fiasco?'

Now it is 2017, the *Forum* has been reconvened, and George Pell has been joined on the podium by his close friend, Tony Abbott, whose brief stint as Prime Minister turned Australia rightward, failing miserably.

Abbott's reign as Prime Minister was just two years. It had been cut short in 2015, but he continues to champion a fossil-fuel burning platform.

The man who once told the populace he would "shirtfront" Vladimir Putin is always ready to take on the green lobby, making more headlines along the way.

'Beware of the pronouncement "the science is settled", Abbott is informing a London gathering.

'It's the spirit of the Inquisition, the thought-police down the ages, rails the man who is known as the "Mad Monk", in some circles.

Abbott is attracting more thinkers critical of him every day.

Writing in the August 2018 issue of revered political and arts magazine, *The Monthly*, liberal journalist Paddy Manning has described Tony Abbott as "the most destructive politician of our time (who) went on to launch a misogynistic campaign against our first female prime minister."

"The failed priest…has done incalculable damage to this country," says Manning, provoking a local movement that will see Tony Abbott lose his seat to climate-change Independent, Zali Steggall, knocking off the ex-PM's 20% majority to a loud cheer squad; ever since Federation, the blue-ribbon prize of Warringah had been an untouchable, conservative stronghold.

But Abbott had misread the electorate. When, after three-quarters of Warringah's constituents voted "Yes" in the Australian Marriage Law Postal Survey on legalising same-sex marriage, he voted against it in the Parliament, the *Vote Tony Out* messaging began appearing on the local streets all the way to election day in 2019.

"The future belongs to those who hear it coming," David Bowie said (reprising the Greek, Heraclitus).

Both Abbott and Pell had ignored the warning, but the latter's backroom mischief-making against the Pope is about to be placed on pause, with the news that a pair of Victorian detectives are on their way to Rome, with questions for George Pell that will rock the Catholic Church off its axis.

<><>

2017
Back in the Dock

'After Sunday Mass, you planted yourself between the two choir boys and the door. The boys knew they were in trouble.'

George Pell being interviewed on camera in his second Rome interview.

He is familiar with the two Victorian detectives: they have been chasing the Cardinal for years, had spoken briefly on a previous occasion remotely. George Pell has been advised to have a lawyer with him.

The detectives have their backs to the camera and are unidentified; one is heard to say, 'You have moved your robes to one side and exposed your penis.'

'Oh, stop it!' cries Pell. 'Disgraceful. What a load of disgraceful rubbish,' he says angrily. 'Completely false – madness,' says Pell.

He has been caught unawares. 'All sorts of people come to the sacristy after Mass,' he says, fumbling hastily to find the words.

George Pell is ignored, and the detective continues, unabashed: 'It has been alleged you took hold of the choir boy's head and forced it down onto your penis.'

Pell is impassive, silent and unresponsive.

The detective presses on: 'The boys were terrified, and you moved on to the other boy. You told him to take his pants off, and you masturbated him while masturbating yourself.'

Pell pauses and, his face impassive, with just the occasional twitch of an eyebrow, he investigates the far distance – in a manner that David Marr says is reminiscent of Pell's four-hour appearance earlier in the Royal Commission. 'The Cardinal always seemed to be far away.'

He appears to be ever so presciently shaken, before saying finally: 'This – in the sacristy? After Mass?'

Again, he pauses to find the words. 'What a load of rubbish. A falsehood! A deranged falsehood.'

And that's it: with the two detectives having their backs to the camera, we can only imagine them quietly taking up their papers and smiling inwardly: they had got what they had come for.

And here I am, impressed with the detectives' calm persistence while on Pell's home ground.

Although I always seem to be the lone observer – locked inside a personal obsession that had its birth in those words I have never forgotten: 'I need your help.'

I was being asked then to be part of the very clerical crimes that are bringing down the Catholic Church.

But this is different, these terrible proceedings are in graphic detail, and I am aware that, behind the questioning of George Pell – its intensity and determination – was a victim who had spoken out.

And hadn't the Royal Commission stated in its rules of engagement: that "children are to be heard"?

Few psychiatrists know more about paedophilia than Doctor Bob Gordon, whose detailed account of the veracity of "horrors" never forgotten rivals the memories of the Holocaust.

'The memories of Auschwitz are akin to a child who was raped living with the experience for as long as they live,' says a man with a string of letters after his name as long as his arm.

Had not my own experience working alongside the fearsome crusader against child sex abuse on the cusp of the 1990s, Gemma, prepared me – given me the strength and confidence to write this book?

'Will you believe me when I tell you I was raped?' I remember we wrote then.

I remember the image of one of Pope Francis' "little ones" being rolled out beside our roads and on the backs of buses in a campaign designed to out terrible secrets once held; crimes that are at last meeting justice. George Pell, his hierarchy already tarnished by its efforts to put a spoke in the Royal Commission, his efforts to keep compensation for victims low thwarted by new laws.

Pell's Melbourne Response is falling apart. The Fosters had proved that with a little effort, the entity is easily circumnavigated when children are believed, and priests' lies are driven over.

But all is far from just, and now one of the most praiseworthy board members of the Melbourne Response has left in disgust. Professor Patrick Parkinson will later declare the Catholic Church has six times the paedophile cases than all the other Churches combined.

<><>

2016
Enemy Number One

"Is Cardinal Pell the enemy of the Church?"

Australian literary legend and one-time seminarian (who was never ordained), Thomas Keneally AO, asks the question in the cover story of Australia's longtime best-selling magazine, the iconic *Women's Weekly* of May 2016.

"Pell's cold and compassionless performance from Rome may be a catastrophe for the Catholic Church in Australia," writes the National Living Treasure.

"Leaders like Cardinal Pell have done so little to stop marauding and abusive clergy," (and due to that failure) many admirable 'ordinary' priests may never recover their repute."

Later, there's this: "Thirteen Cardinals (led by George Pell) wrote to Pope Francis last October accusing him of putting too many liberal-minded churchmen and laypeople into the synod of bishops which had met in Rome to discuss – the Church's attitude to – 'the family'."

"Pell has never quite seen the urgency of addressing paedophilia as fully as he had attacked the supposed Catholic sins (divorce, contraception, homosexual love) of laypeople.

"Thus, it appears, on his own evidence," the legend writes, "that the Cardinal is more open to paedophile priests consecrating the host and taking Communion than he is to anyone, divorced or gay, whatever their virtues, talents and good will, receiving the host."

And now, the red-hatted cardinals of a men-only hierarchy – that Thomas Keneally's equal in penmanship, Morris West, wrote about in his 1981 best-selling novel, *The Clowns of God* – have been asked *en masse* by Pope Frances to place those *"little ones"* at the centre of the Catholic Church.

There's a time for prayer, and a time for hope. But now Pope Francis and his cabinet of cardinals – the *curia* – is being called to real action.

'In the face of the scourge of the abuse by Churchmen, to the detriment of minors, we hear the cry of victims who ask for justice,' their pope is saying.

'The weight of the pastoral and the Church's responsibility weighs on our meeting. The holy people of God look at us and expect of us not simple and obvious condemnations, but effective and concrete measures be put into place.'

Will this modern pope's demands be heeded? Doubters among the aggrieved find little to agree on, beyond hope.

<><><>

Four

WHEN THE BELL TOLLS, IT RHYMES

2018
Trial of the 21st Century?

George Pell, 'charged with child sexual assault'?

Father Mick says he cannot believe it.

'He is a thug and a bully. But *in church*? After Sunday mass?' he says, referencing the cardinal's previous protestations in the Rome hearing.

That's strange for Mick; but while he can't stand the sight of him, he can't believe the man he insists upon calling 'George', in deprecation of Pell's position in the hierarchy, would be so stupid.

'He is used to getting his own way,' I remind the retired priest, who is anything but traditionalist, and is all for "love" first and foremost, no matter the circumstances. I tell him I once asked Doctor Robert Gordon if he thought Pell might just happen to be a classic psychopath.

'And? What was his answer?'

'He said Pell "definitely displays the tendencies".'

(Thug. Bully. Mick. Has got that right!)

<>

Soon the news is out: that George Pell has been charged with molesting two choir boys in the confines of the Melbourne Cathedral.

Sometime in December 1996.

Three months before, Chrissie and Anthony Foster finally had that brief meeting with Pell when he shamefully misread the truth placed in front of his unsympathetic eyes.

One of the boys, now in his thirties, had been encouraged to come forward, after following the horrors that emerged in the Royal Commission.

The police had taken his depositions to the Rome interviews.

The young man is the only survivor of those rapes; his friend having died by suicide.

George Pell is required to turn up in a Victorian court within weeks.

The news is that Pope Francis has cut him loose financially.

Pell has lost his job in the inner circle of the College of Cardinals.

George Pell is in rarefied air.

<>

Pell is on his own; and from all reports, he remains unperturbed and will rely on his usual coterie of wealthy supporters.

Fisher is already asking congregations in the NSW dioceses to stump up for the cardinal's legal bills – that are already being touted as expected to be 'in the millions'.

The Sydney Archbishop owes his post to George Pell and is out on the hustings, accusing the press of being 'always after Cardinal Pell, and the Church'.

'Crucify him! Crucify him!' In an attempt to win favour with the faithful, Fisher is claiming an echo of two thousand years ago.'Those words are as relevant today as they were when the rabble demanded Jesus' life,' Fisher says, with undisguised empathy for his mentor.

Being in charge of St Mary's Cathedral, Archbishop Fisher is responsible for the crypt, wherein reside the heavy sandstone tombs of all the cathedral's cardinals.

<><>

2018
The Witness is to be Believed

They're out in force: Pell's supporters have grasped the word in sections of the world's media as evidence the cardinal won't get a fair hearing and it has increased their determination to protect the Church – by protecting their man – no matter how tight the evidence, regardless of the verdict, and with no concern about what it costs.

Admittedly, hypothesising about the Catholic Church being on trial here is supported by its recent history and the past two popes' failure to recognise the litany of horrors of the sexual abuse of children by countless priests.

There had been the autocratic Pole's mishandling of Boston Cardinal Benjamin Law who had kept hidden the crimes of hundreds of abusive priests (recent Church documents reveal that he had known one of the priests had raped and molested some 130 of the city's innocents).

Pope John Paul II had "rewarded" Law's criminal activity with the coveted post of archpriest of Rome's largest Marian church, the Basilica di Santa Maria Maggiore, a coveted position the Boston hierarch held tightly until he resigned his Vatican posting, aged 80.

The same pope had protected his money-making friend and leader of the now-defunct *Legionnaires*, Father Marcial Maciel, who had molested dozens of young children, of both sexes, encouraging his men to engage in orgies; while he himself is known to have fathered at least two children, the mothers often paid off, left to bring the children up as orphans.

(Dublin Jesuit Father Peter Byrne describes Maciel in *The Tablet* as a "sociopath" and "gangster").

Neither Cardinal Law nor Maciel were ever brought to trial, and both died as free men at great ages in the comfort of their own beds; Law in Rome in 2017 and the Legionnaires' head twelve years earlier. After a 60-year "career" of sexually abusing the young, Maciel had come to end his days living a "quiet life" in the United States.

<>

It was the Church's problem with child sexual abuse that brought about Pope Benedict XVI's abdication in 2013 – cogently fictionalised in the movie, *The Two Popes* – "due to ill health" and the installing of Jorge Bergoglio as Pope Francis.

Pope Benedict/Joseph Ratzinger's protecting of the Catholic Church will be laid bare in 2022 when the release of a long-awaited "German Report" will detail 235 priest abusers in that country, involving at least 497 children. Some of their molesters even denied requests to leave the priesthood, due to the lack of priests. Their crimes were covered up by Ratzinger, both as bishop and pope.

<>

George Pell's trial soon finds me revisiting the Vatican's indifference to those brave victims who approach it seeking compensation and demanding answers.

Ian Lawther: technically blind since the fateful day he set out to murder the priest who had groomed his son for sexual gratification.

Ian tells me he hopes that the brave young man 'witnessing against Cardinal Pell will know that many like me and my son, Stephen, will be with him every step of the way'.

Pell's accuser is already up against it, with the cardinal's die-hard supporters citing the lack of witnesses to the alleged rape. A common defensive ploy in *"his word against mine'"* trials, it will be tested in the Australian High Court.

<>

'This is no "celebrity trial",' cries my ex-Catholic friend, Nick, in an echo of many media stories. 'Pell is no "celebrity",' he says scornfully.

'But it's the trial of the century,' he adds, after a sip of coffee, and reminds me of the part I once played in Catholicism's betrayal of the innocents.

I reminded Nick that had the secretive one-on-one meeting I had endured with the Marist leader became known, 'I would have been seen to be complicit in a crime.'

'The first chapter of your book is called MEA CULPA,' he says with emphasis. 'I told you to stop beating yourself up then.'

'I hope that hasn't been lost. After all this time,' he adds, with a rueful smile.

Pausing, I am soon reminding my lapsed-Catholic friend that I will live with those words until I die.

'They're my shame, Nick. I was forced to keep a terrible secret.'

Nick thinks before he speaks: 'But, now you can write about it.'

'Yes. I'm pleased you agree,' I say. He is right behind me, wanting to read more.

He says he can help with some stories of his own. 'With my time in the '50s. At "Joey's".'

'Paedophilia at that "esteemed" college,' he says, 'is not confined to more recent times, you know.'

He presents a slightly twisted smile, and orders toast and more coffees from the waiter who has been hovering. She is young and pretty, and appears to be far from worldly, but says, 'Sounds like your book is something I need to read. Sounds important.'

'I hope it is published,' she says, and has our full attention.

No more than a girl, she has kind eyes; but the dark shadows beneath belie an inner truth that I expect is not about to be revealed to us.

'I hope you won't be the only one,' I say sheepishly, and hope she hadn't noticed I had been studying her, before she walks away.

Nick returns to the book. 'And I hope you aren't going easy on Pell,' he says with a sideways look that catches another interested party, before he makes an announcement that he might have been saving up for this moment.

'Whatever is coming to *Cardinal* Pell,' Nick says loudly, 'the bastard deserves every bit of it. George Pell is an evil prick,' he declares uncharacteristically, setting me back with its derision.

Nick then presents a wry smile, and says Pell is one of the reasons a Catholic Church won't be seeing him anytime soon. 'I don't expect, ever,' he says.

'I know I am judging before *Cardinal* Pell is tried,' he says, before tossing his arms about in a futile way.

We both know Pell's supporters are hoping more people have reached such a conclusion.

<>

Nick is suddenly pensive.

'We knew Brother Stephen was buggering our classmates,' he says revealingly.

'And now?'

'Well, Cardinal Pell is the last straw for me. I don't need more reason to leave the Catholic Church. Say goodbye forever,' says Nick, and he is instantly thoughtful once more. 'Of course, my wife is an atheist,' he says with a rueful smile.

'Don't worry,' I say, 'The Cardinal' – Nick flinches at the word – 'George Pell is now in justice's headlights, and we can only hope justice is served.'

'The Catholic Church will fight back,' Nick says, with forlorn hope. The Vatican has always been blind to the raping of kids.'

I can only nod to that. 'But speak to rusted-on *tykes* and it's a different story: almost to a man – it is not so much the women, strangely – and you'll find far too many believe it is the *Church* that's on trial.'

Tykes. Nick smiles grimly at my use of a word to describe Catholics that would have been derogatory when he was young.

'What "Church"?' he cries. 'The one I grew up with has been stolen. By people like George Pell.'

Pausing briefly, Nick says lamentably, 'But you weren't born *tyke*. It's not in your blood. And wouldn't matter as much.'

'That so? I say, remembering a year I once spent badgering a well-known communist and the extraordinary Jesuit I once spent time with, when we'd be discussing their differences, as well as their sameness; but that's for later in this book.

<>

And that's where we leave off and begin talking about the Ashes Test later this year, when we will take our seats in the Noble Stand, behind the bowler's arm, and dine on Nick's boiled eggs and cheese sandwiches, and later the fruit cake his barrister friend never fails to bring along.

The lawyer tells me he has joined our mate in leaving the Church he grew up in.

More pity the Catholic Church: it's losing its intellectuals.

Scientists, writers, teachers, lawyers, too many to count; add them to the thousands of ordinary folks who, while many of us remain in the Jesus Church, won't be darkening the doors of the *institutional* Church anytime soon.

Pope Francis might be a remarkable reformist but the remarkable "Frankie" – as Father Mick is fond of calling him – is struggling to fix the Catholic Church's biggest problem since the Reformation.

The only religion discussed at the cricket will be what's in front of us.

Will it be a typical SCG pitch? One in which spin takes the wickets – especially on the last day?

Ever since Warnie, we have admired the artifice of the slow bowler more than the quicks.

Especially on a turning wicket at the SCG.

<><>

2018
He's Coming Home

The Rome interviews are on *YouTube*, word by devastating word, and are joined on the internet by Australian favourite, Tim Minchin.

Famous for the musical, *Matilda*, Minchin has penned a timely song:

> *Come home, Cardinal Pell,*
> *Come down from your citadel.*
> *I'm sure they'll make you*
> *Feel welcome.*
> *At the pub in Ballarat,*
> *They just want a beer and a chat.*

<>

Pell has reached the retiring age for hierarchs, 75, but it appears any thought of that has been put on hold; at least until his legal matter is settled.

Don't you worry, Tim Minchin: George Pell is "coming home".

In good news for victims, the ribbons that have long decorated church fences in Ballarat and Melbourne have been refreshed. A "rainbow fence" marking the hundreds of child rapes that took place in those confines.

George Pell's alleged abuses and cover-ups mostly took place in Ballarat and before the subject of these current proceedings that the prosecution alleges happened in the Church's highest Victorian precinct, Melbourne's St Patrick's Cathedral.

While the cardinal appears to be proud and determined, those qualities also come with an arrogant disregard for the secular law that Pell sees as inferior to *Church* law.

Whether he has been ordered to return to Melbourne by the pope, or is coming on his own volition, there's credit to be had in the plaintiff's decision to face the music.

Unlike the cowardly examples of Washington's Cardinal Thomas McCarrick, and Boston's infamous Bernard Law, Pell will have his day in court.

McCarrick and Law live quietly in Rome, along with their guilt and shame. Mother Church their protector, that duo are safe under the Vatican's diplomatic status that has allegedly helped to protect tax criminals, money launderers, Mafia figures and many others of ill repute over many decades.

<>

Pell's reckoning is an astonishing outcome for the small band of survivors and supporters who have maintained an ominous vigil during the Rome interview; Chrissie and Anthony Foster had been there and while it is less than a year since Anthony's untimely death from a stroke, Chrissie's iron resolve remains undaunted in her quest for a mother's justice from a cruel, unmoving Church.

The Catholic Church might be the protector of the faith, but Pell's arraignment on the very crimes he has made a career of covering up has caught both survivors and the cardinal's supporters off guard.

And while many are forced to watch from afar, a handpicked crew will be allowed into the court.

Chrissie Foster's high profile has gained her a coveted spot inside, together with select journalists, including Pell biographer, Louise Milligan.

Milligan's best-seller, *Cardinal, The Rise and Fall of George Pell*, along with Chrissie's *Hell on the Way to Heaven* are top of mind once more.

The Jesuit priest and writer, Frank Brennan, will be in the court as a representative of the Church.

And so will Francis Sullivan, who is a broken man from doing the Church's bidding over the compensation problem created for him by the man on trial.

As for the accused, it is hard to believe but recent government initiatives mean there is more at stake for George Pell than can be at first assumed.

The cardinal could lose other freedoms, besides jail.

The past year saw the federal government of Prime Minister Malcolm Turnbull pass a law cancelling the passports of known *paedophiles.*

Paedophiles are to have their names placed on a register, for children's protection.

Both add weight to the continuing cries from certain quarters that Pell may not get a fair trial.

There's one man who will be determined that he does.

<><>

2018
A Man of Substance and Singularity

Judge Peter Kidd (AO) is a perfect choice to try the errant cardinal.

Three years prosecuting at the War Crimes Tribunal in Bosnia – the horrors there unimaginable – have helped produce a lawman of forensically painstaking abilities and with the patience of Job in the pursuit of justice.

Fears that we are about to see a "celebrity" trial disappear in the ether when the first sitting day sees Judge Kidd declare the court is to be closed to the Australian media 'until all matters are finalised'.

That will be the last Australians will hear about the trial of George Pell for some time.

Yet, while the local news blackout under Victoria's suppression laws is effective in gagging news of the trial, it hasn't stopped the Melbourne Herald-Sun from plastering a single word on its front page:

"CENSORED"

The same day sees this from *The Sydney Morning Herald*: "While the world is reading a very important story that is relevant to Victorians, we are prevented from publishing details of this significant news. But trust us. It's a story you deserve to read."

And, as the paper implies, it hasn't proved difficult to do so.

Not with the blackout confined only to Australia.

Not for anyone with a computer and an internet connection:

"The boys sang in the choir at St Patrick's Cathedral and were abused by Pell in a room in the confines of the Church," trumpets international news website, *The Daily Beast.*

That's just one; others in the overseas media contingent are following the same lines.

But while Chrissie Foster is saying, 'There is always suspicion when you don't know what is going on,' it will be the facts that matter, and Australians won't be hearing what's going on behind those closed doors for five months.

While the trial has been framed by the recent parliamentary apology to victims of child sexual abuse, the background noise will be compelling, and George Pell is going to need all the help he can get.

<>

The Cardinal's choice of barrister is, in that regard, quite a surprise.

If, as the tactic implies, the aim is not so much to prove Pell's innocence, as to "get him off".

"The mobster's silk": that's how Robert Richter QC has been described in various quarters.

"Loud and an avowed atheist…not the obvious choice to defend Cardinal George Pell against historical sex charges," writes Sydney's Tim Elliott in a *Herald* feature. "But the celebrity silk's reputation for skewering witnesses – and winning cases – has delivered him the most high-profile case in his long, storied career."

'Got Mick Gatto off, he did,' I am told is bandied about the criminal fraternity.

The facts in that case are that it was on self-defence: "After the infamous gangland leader forced his would-be assassin's gun to turn back onto him and kept firing until the man dropped. Whose finger was on the trigger?" Elliott writes of Gatto's canny barrister asking the court.

Amazed at his good fortune, the gangland leader had his barrister's name tattooed across his torso.

"A hoodlum's mark of respect," writes Elliott.

But, not done yet, Pell's by now infamous QC had gone on to get another killer off, charged with shooting his neighbour after an argument. Richter told the court the dead man had been 'leaning on a menacing shovel at the time'.

There was the case of the man with a child on his knee who drove a ute into a crowd, killing seven: Richter had the sentence reduced from 20 years to 10 on appeal. Now, the credentialled Robert Richter QC is to defend George Pell – a fee reportedly in the order of $10,000 to $15,000 per day.

<>

So: who is Robert Richter QC?

According to journalist Tim Elliott, Richter appears as "slightly scruffy in the legal attire of black cassock and tired grey wig, the old-fashioned 'penguin' look".

The photo of Richter I am staring at is of a tired face, tatty grey beard, thinning white hair combed to the side, mouth half-open in anticipation and with large ears that would be prominent too, were they not pressed hard against Richter's head, like a rugby no. 2 who has been in too many scrums; his forehead is high, with a perpetual frown, and the whole speaks of the weariness of long experience.

While the eyes staring out of the page disguise an almost certain cunning, they also reflect that sense of vulnerability that often wins juries over.

Robert Richter QC is obviously clever and determined.

His biography, as told by Tim Elliott in *Good Weekend Magazine* in February 2018, begins with Richter being born in the murderous Stalin times; when after escaping, the young boy spent his early years in a German refugee camp before the family went to Israel, later arriving in Australia. It was a situation that the boy immediately found to be "miserable", his word at the time for their chosen country.

Richter turned out to be bright, topped the university rankings, set about specialising in crime and became one of the most skilled and notorious barristers in the nation.

Now he is running the trial of his life.

An international celebrity he will be, and he doesn't pull punches in announcing himself to the eager media.

He is forthright: 'I just wanted it to be known, straight off, that this is not one of those cases where he is going to lie down. The Cardinal has been set up to fall by people who know nothing about the actual charges. He is innocent and he needs help.'

<><>

2018
The Accusations

So, it turns out that the Victorian detectives' purpose in Rome had been to pursue allegations by a young man with a story to tell that would rock the Catholic Church to its very soul.

Encouraged by the horrors outed in the Royal Commission, Pell's accuser is now in his thirties.

His allegation that both he and a fellow choir boy had been raped by George Pell in the sacristy of Melbourne's Catholic cathedral – the actions had allegedly taken place in 1997 – comes with a tragic twist.

One that helps to explain why this courageous 35-year-old has thrown caution to the wind, and demands truth be heard, and justice fairly met.

After struggling to move beyond the pain of the memory, the boy's friend had died of a drug overdose, prompting his friend to act.

There is much to be applauded about this brave young man. He knows he is up against a beast of great power who, like the Caesars of old, is feared by many in the Catholic Church, and revered as a man that the philosopher H. L. Mencken described as being of a rank "above other human beings".

'Is the priest *God?*' my seven-year-old granddaughter had once asked, the young beauty's innocent eyes transfixed by the priest in all his finery solemnly saying the Mass.

Truth from the mouth of a babe, they are the scariest words I have ever heard.

Shaken to my core, was my meekly constructed reply enough?

'No, darling, he's just a man, like me.'

Let us have more humanity and less of God!

<>

The cardinal's accuser knows that he and George Pell are the only people alive who remember what has been alleged took place more than two decades ago in the Melbourne Catholic cathedral.

But the death of the young man's friend has made him steadfast; he is undaunted.

He has already been through the taxing moments of George Pell's committal trial and Pell's attack dog shouting: 'You're a liar! *A liar.*'

Many in the courtroom that day must have felt their reaction vindicated when the magistrate had sufficient belief in the testimony to hand Pell's fate to "twelve and true".

Now, Judge Kidd has given the young man a cover for his own protection: his name will never be known, under the law of the land.

"Witness J" carries on his strong shoulders all those who have been denied justice from the Catholic Church.

But in his mind, there will always be one above all others, who is more important than him.

"He has lain down his life for his friend." (*Greater love has no man than...* John 15:13)

<><>

2018
The "Loud" Fence

Few places on Earth have seen hurt more over the decades by the deafening silence from Catholic Church indifference to the pattern of criminal sexual behaviour against a city's children than troubled Ballarat: 26 have been lost to suicide.

But the news locals have been waiting for about their one-time resident, whose appearance in the Commission has already brought instant fame to their city where gold is still mined, and ever since the 1956 Olympics rowing championships still held. Many locals have manned the fence outside Bathurst's own St Patrick's Cathedral for years; its iron railings festooned with clean, coloured ribbons in recognition of the hurt inflicted on Ballarat's children. Their vigil speaks with a loud voice in an ominous silence.

A city of less than 100,000, Ballarat rivals Boston for priests' crimes and it is 20 years since victims had first tied a rainbow of coloured ribbons to the cathedral fences, their defiant message resonating around the world.

One for each victim, an unconscionable number spelt out, *twenty-six* – that it is said has recently swelled to 27 – of Ballarat's young ones, disciples in the spirit, crucified.

Maureen Hatcher, the initiative's founder, explains: 'The guys from Scotland contacted me, to see if we would support them (in the cause against child-abuse crimes in that country), as they are doing a three-day, three-night vigil.'

Cardinal Pell's trial was recognised from across the world.

The Church had taken the ribbons down numerous times; only to see them replaced overnight, by heart-driven Banksy.

But they haven't been taken down since February and the advent of the Pell trial, when dozens of sympathisers joined in replacing those ribbons. The "Loud

Fence" has become a story also broadcast worldwide.

They live in hope, silently preparing to give voice in "one minute of noise" when the result they hope for, pray for, will see the law finally wield the axe upon George Pell, after multiple hearings and a pre-trial Inquiry.

The eerie sound of bagpipes will fill the air across the hemispheres in anticipation of the most important chapter of the Church's betrayal so far – Pell gone to jail.

Many of Ballarat's finest had once joined other survivors and supporters and journeyed to Rome for the now legendary Pell interview, and while eager for that guilty verdict, they remain certain of one thing: he knew. Knew what had been going on in Ballarat, both while he was there, and after.

Broken Rites has more to say about Ballarat than anywhere else and confirms Church leaders had ignored what was going on at their primary school in Ballarat during the 1970s for years.

"But we knew (for example) that a band of four Christian Brothers had been regularly abusing boys as young as 7 at (the school) St Alipius."

Interestingly, in a Church that loves its saints, Alipius doesn't get a mention (although there is a St Alypius, who is curiously described as "a helper, or intercessor with infertility").

More damning is the fact that the school chaplain in those years was George Pell's friend and number one supporter, the notorious Father Gerald Ridsdale. Pell had been pleased to champion Ridsdale, a serial offender for more than three decades, and a fateful day in 1993 saw an auspicious newspaper photo beamed around the world: of the serially abusing priest in heavy dark glasses being accompanied by his bishop, George Pell.

Four years after accompanying his friend to court, it will be alleged Pell's own crimes took place, and many are asking: is the Pell/Ridsdale connection – its headlining by the Royal Commission – the catalyst for the hierarch's accuser to come forth with his allegations that he and his fellow choirboy were molested by George Pell in Melbourne's Saint Patrick's Cathedral?

Gerald Ridsdale and Pell's other close friend, the priest O'Donnell, who molested the Foster girls, were two of the Catholic Church's most notorious child abusers, but seemingly protected species when under the care of George Pell.

<>

'I look forward to many, many more years of work from Father Kevin O'Donnell in the Church here,' Pell said of one of the worst of the worst.

The year was 1988 and Pell had recently been made bishop – Mencken's "a species superior to other human beings" – and was speaking to a confirmation celebration in Melbourne.

Broken Rites says the Church must have known O'Donnell was a sex abuser at the time, as many had been alerting its authorities for years.

"Since he was ordained, in 1942."

So: a serial abuser of at least 50 young children, Father O'Donnell had managed to "fit Masses, weddings and funerals in between his sex-abuse activities," the website says.

The Church had ignored the crimes of one of its most dangerous priests for over four decades: Pell unconscionably placing more weight on O'Donnell's consummate expertise in more temporal matters. O'Donnell shared George Pell's deft hand at finance, prompting Pell to say of his "two a day" friend: 'Father Kevin O'Donnell's dealings in real estate were legendary.'

He said O'Donnell had set up a retirement home for the clergy.

Known by other priests to be a "Pell man", *Broken Rites* says when alerted to their fellow cleric's crimes, "they didn't want to know about it".

Pell had looked after O'Donnell; they were two peas in the same financial pod "from day one".

Broken Rites says Pell had the friend he lauded over placed in a tomb reserved for the Catholic Church's most notable priests.

Above his name, the words *Priest emeritus.*

A monster of the Church – "retired with honour".

The "celebration" of O'Donnell's life was the closest the Church ever came to a state funeral.

<>

The number of children Father Gerald Ridsdale assaulted through a lifetime of abuse has not been finally tallied, but when sentenced to a further 11 years in 2017, the list of his known abuses had grown to 161.

The judge said then: 'Your actions were violent and abusive. You shared your position of power and trust over each of your complainants. You knew what you were doing was wrong. You knew no boundaries, on occasion offending in your church, in the confessional, in your presbyteries.'

One of Ridsdale's five trials heard of a little girl being stripped naked and raped on the altar of a Ballarat church, after which "he wiped away her tears, told her he loved her, and gave her a bag of boiled lollies".

Victims who were in court that day said they hoped their abuser would die in jail.

"EVEN HELL TOO GOOD FOR EVIL PRIEST," headlined Melbourne's *Herald-Sun*.

Evil in the Catholic Church, its lack of empathy and compassion at such times rampant under the likes of leaders such as then Bishop George Pell.

<><>

2018
Ridsdale's Nephew Speaks

'Fuck you, George, and everything you stand for.'

An angry David Ridsdale, speaking of a conversation he had with Pell in 1995 about the uncle who had molested him.

Father Gerald Ridsdale often took young David on holidays when he had successfully groomed the lonely little boy for the purpose of abusing him.

David Ridsdale says Pell had later phoned him out of the blue.

But soon his purpose became clear.

'George (Pell) began to talk about my growing family and my need to take care of their needs,' he told the Royal Commission.

'He mentioned how I would soon have to buy a car or a house for my family. I remember with clarity the last three lines we spoke together. I said: "Excuse me George, what are you talking about?" He said he wanted to know what it would take to keep me quiet.'

'And that's when I said: "Fuck you George and everything you stand for."'

Pell admitted he didn't provide any help to his colleague's victim.

'But I did regard him as a friend,' the cardinal told the Royal Commission that had recently heard another of Father Gerald Ridsdale's victims testify that he was told what the priest was doing to him was 'God's work', and 'bad things will happen to your family if you don't do as I wish'.

<>

David Ridsdale's experience had him determined to seek justice for all victims and he helped coordinate the group of survivors who went to Rome.

'We waited in great hope (that Pell's grilling remotely by the Royal Commission) would find him charged by the police, at least for his multiple cover-ups.'

Paul Levey was in Rome with that contingent of hopefuls – having been one of those Ballarat boys who survived, and he speaks of Father Ridsdale often having boys in his bed.

'He had groomed a lonely Ballarat lad with obvious family problems, by taking the boy from his parents to live with him in the presbytery.'

Levey said the priest had the boy with him for six months.

He says, in all that time, the Church authorities had remained aloof.

While the local bishop said he 'didn't know paedophilia is a crime'.

'Not really, Bishop Mulkearns repeated later.

'Mulkearns was unconcerned to protect children from these priests,' Levey says.

<>

Ronald Mulkearns was "retired" prematurely, receiving a bishop's generous stipend and other perks of hierarchs in the Catholic Church.

He died in 2016, soon after the completion of his compatriot George Pell's first Rome hearings.

Aged 86, he had avoided scrutiny of his cover-ups; and yet he once told the Commission: 'The sexual abuse of children is a problem with priests.'

Confession in a born-Catholic's blood, let those words be the epitaph of Bishop Ronald Mulkearns.

<>

Chrissie Foster was in court the day a Ballarat survivor held up a class photo of 33 boys from the St Alipius school.

'Twelve had been tellingly highlighted. They had all died by suicide," she said.

Meanwhile, survivors are carefully tying and retying the ribbons on St Alipius' *Loud Fence*, in tandem with the 'guys from Scotland'.

Ballarat must surely rival Boston as the paedophilia capital of the Catholic world.

<>

It's the 15th of August 2018, and due to the suppression order, what is taking place can't be reported.

Unless you are overseas.

Although, when it is finally revealed, Australians will also know that after a month of evidence, the jury was unable to reach a verdict.

Justice Kidd orders a new trial to begin immediately before a jury of 12 and true.

The four-month trial is quick in the scheme of such things, and the jury will deliberate for just four days, returning a unanimous verdict on 11 December, 2018.

George Pell guilty, and on all five charges.

This prompts Richter QC to announce he will appeal – 'absolutely we will' – also asking for bail, so the cardinal can have a knee reconstruction.

Justice Kidd grants the bail on strict conditions, and George Pell, child molester, will be free – perhaps not quite "as a bird" – until the end of February, 2019.

Two days after the verdict, Pope Francis will remove the Australian from his inner circle of advisors, the new Privy Council.

Described politically as 'a major restructure', Pell retains his position on the Holy See's Treasury where his forensic abilities, paired with his well-known bullying tactics, had enjoyed success in finding much of the Church's missing millions.

But it will be two more months before Australians will learn about all this, when, after prosecutors fail in having their argument that George Pell had a "tendency" to molest boys in swimming pools admitted as evidence, and one of their key witnesses in that matter had died, Justice Kidd will lift the suppression order.

With the local media already impatient, their pencils poised and cameras readied, Richter QC wasn't going to waste the opportunity to insert himself into their scrum.

<><>

2019
Richter's Comment

George Pell has been found guilty on all five counts of molesting two choirboys in the confines of Melbourne Catholic Cathedral, St Patrick's. His barrister, Robert Richter QC, was on the steps of the County Court of Victoria. It is the 23rd of February, 2019.

Desperate for a reprieve of his own reputation, George Pell's principal lawman stretches credibility when he describes his client's alleged forcing of one child's mouth onto his exposed penis as being 'seized by some terrible impulse'.

The Cardinal's alleged masturbation of the other boy and himself, Richter describes as 'a fleeting touch'.

He says his client is a man infected with a great deal of passion. He has a great sense of humour.'

"Funny" wasn't the word for it when the cardinal allegedly used his power to corner the boys in the sacristy and began fumbling under his robes.

'You're in trouble,' Pell had allegedly said to the frightened boys.

<>

We later learned that one young man in the witness box had bravely withstood a merciless grilling for two-and-a-half days by a black-and-white clad posse of bewigged legals costing more than $20,000 a day.

Their sole mission? To pull apart the testimony of one lone human being, there not just for himself, but primarily for the ghost who was beside him all the way; Witness J's inner moral strength and drive to seek justice had left the young man no option but to speak out

Testament to truth, there's hope other victims will be encouraged to come forward, tell their stories and have justice served.

Robert Richter QC might have got the notorious gangland boss, Mick Gatto, off on a murder charge. But he couldn't break that courageous young man, once in the pre-trial committal court and then again before two juries, the first trial declared a mistrial, while the second trial had seen George Pell found guilty in a unanimous verdict.

Justice Kidd had directed the juries to concentrate on the charges, and "not make a scapegoat of the Catholic Church," the respected online *Guardian Australia* newspaper is saying.

When George Pell's legal team had its appeal turned down by the Victorian Supreme Court in a 2-to-1 judge majority, it was the last hurrah for Robert Richter QC.

But it heralded a new day for the Catholic Church and Pope Francis' "little ones".

Pell was not expected to have the name of his silk tattooed across his pecs any time soon.

<>

Meanwhile, in a small Catholic church in far-flung Western Australia, a popular priest is greeting the few stragglers who have remained part of his dwindling congregation, despite the church's greatest crisis since the Reformation.

'Thanks so much for coming to Mass,' he says to each and every one of them, shaking their hands in turn.

Jesus had not been on trial in their eyes, and neither their sense of community; they are Christians in the spirit of the original Church, St Irenaeus's "the people of God" that Pope Francis has set his mind to rebuilding in justice and fairness; it is a move that could stop the flow of leavers and save the Catholic Church – from itself.

A new Church built upon the ashes of the paedophilia crimes that have brought the Catholic Church to its knees, such small gatherings with their modern priests represent the communal remnants that can save the Jesus religion, with its origin in mercy, love and pity, from oblivion.

The Ides of March, the 1st, have arrived, and *The Saturday Paper's* Alex McKinnon writes: "For nearly 20 years, the Australian Catholic Church's response to child sexual abuse was shaped by a child molester."

<><><>

Five

HOW THE MIGHTY FALL

2019
George Pell is Sentenced

Wednesday, March 13: I haven't slept much. I expect I am but one of many who have been forced onto "Pell watch"; long focused on the Catholic Church's betrayal of its most vulnerable.

Children, molested in their thousands, while the Church slept through it.

But now there's hope that at least George Pell's sentencing will send a warning to others.

Pope Francis – unlike his predecessors, especially Benedict XVI - had at least acknowledged the Church has a 'clerical problem', manifested perhaps in Francis' cutting George Pell loose. But the pope's critics are still hoping he is not "all talk", and Pell's sentencing will change the narrative and go some way to saving the institutional Church from its ruination.

<>

I have risen, at 5am and headed to the beach where the 'Huey' God is beginning to reveal himself in the sun's first rays creeping above the far horizon; soon it will lightly touch the waves, white flicks of light dancing in the air.

There's been a pain in my heart since rising; it's beating loudly in the deafening silence.

A small, lone surfer is a shadow on the tide's edge. A small boy, I hope his innocence will never be brutally taken away, as George Pell's alleged victims had been.

Time passes: I must have dozed off; because when I look up, the young surfie is far out in the water. He has been joined by others, older, they'll keep an eye on the grommet; but they won't take too kindly to him "stealing" their waves. Cheekiness is a common trait among the brave and foolhardy youth of the surfing brigade; and, after watching them catch a few waves, I venture into the water myself. The white board at the surf club had promised 22 degrees, and I swim a bit, before I am lying on my back like a turtle, watching wispy clouds drift by.

I am restless, of course, and impatient that the jury's "will be done". Some are saying it's a sad day for the Catholic Church – and well it might be, but I find the thought reprehensible: it's about the *children*, for God's sake.

It has always been about children, and now it's their time.

But all Pell-crony Fisher has to say in the time of giving is a rant about government moves to bring Catholicism's unique and secret confession lore under the law of the land. While we're hearing from the Anglican's Bishop Davies that he too has issue with government that wants to stop him kicking gays out of its schools.

None of Pope Francis' 'Who am I to judge?' to see there.

The pope had already ordered clerics under his watch to break "the cone of silence" and notify the police upon hearing someone confess to being a child molester. No more cover up: priests who have sexually abused children must be turned over to the police.

They must face 'human justice and prepare for divine justice,' said Pope Francis in his Christmas message three months earlier.

Deadly serious reports in *The New York Times* are that the Vatican has defrocked the retired Washington Cardinal Theodore McCarrick.

Relieved of his duties in July, McCarrick had faced a Vatican trial in the Holy See, whereupon he was found to be guilty of several "sins" including "abuse of power…soliciting sex during confession" and "sins with minors and with adults".

"The move appears to be the first time any cardinal has been defrocked for sexual abuse – marking a critical moment in the Vatican's handling of a scandal that has gripped the Church for nearly two decades," opines the *New York Times*.

"It is also the first time an American cardinal has been removed from the priesthood. "He preyed on young men who wanted to become priests; then he became a cardinal," declared one of the world's most respected newspapers.

"One of those young men said he was 11 when an abusive relationship began," says the *Times'* report in which a victim grieves, "For years I have suffered, as many others have, at the hands of Theodore McCarrick (and) it is with profound sadness that I have had to participate in the canonical trial of my abuser. Nothing can give me back my childhood."

"With that said, I am happy that the Pope believed me. I am hopeful now that I can pass through my anger for the last time. I hope that Cardinal McCarrick will no longer be able to use the power of Jesus' Church to manipulate families and sexually abuse children."

The pope called a summit on child sexual abuse that is due to commence almost immediately.

But would it be enough when I am told defrocking is not even excommunication? Nor, due to the statute of limitations present in Washington State at the time, had McCarrick faced the law in his United States home.

<>

George Pell had faced the law.

Finally. And his sentencing has come. I towel myself off; the beach café is open. I grab a takeaway coffee and head home. Helen and I will come back later, walk the beach to its end, where we'll touch a rock in acknowledgement of its existence in the nature of things – before trekking a second half an hour back.

We watch our steps: the sea can be tricky, as we found one day recently when, engrossed in conversation, we had lost our footing, the outgoing tide taking us out, along with my phone and Helen's handbag.

'Huey' dumped us back on the beach along with all our possessions that day.

And now we hope God is listening on this most ominous of days.

Judge Peter Kidd had said (Cardinal) George Pell would be sentenced later.

He could face up to 14 years in jail.

Pell could only appeal after sentencing; and even then, revisiting the verdict could be entertained only on "technical grounds".

The Cardinal's name had been on everyone's lips, and planes packed with journalists had flown in from every corner of the globe, zooming in on Melbourne's biggest spectacle since Michelle Payne had earlier won the Cup in 2015.

Meanwhile, outsiders of all stripes remain hopeful George Pell will also be brought to justice for the serial cover-ups and multiple suicides of victims that had taken place under his watch over many decades.

Twenty-six in one Australian city alone.

Suffer the "little ones".

<>

I have important phone calls to make.

Ever since Ian Lawther had told me his horrific story, we speak regularly and when I reach him, he says he was about to call me.

'It's a big day for victims,' I say.

'The biggest,' he says. But he hopes Pell in jail won't be the end of it. 'There's all the other priests Cardinal Pell protected.'

'Where are you?'

He says he is 'with the others'. The enduring group of victims and supporters. 'Chrissie is here, and Judy Courtin' – Ms Courtin that dedicated lawyer whose busy schedule involves clerical crimes almost exclusively – they are all there for each other; always have been.

Never give up on truth.

Judge Kidd has killed off media controversy by allowing cameras into his court, whereupon Australians will be watching the fate of one of the Catholic Church's highest-ranking hierarchs unfold on *ABC* national television, the rest of the world confined to YouTube, in the judge's determination that all will know the law hadn't been intimidated or interfered with by those with a mind – and the money – to do so.

I am in it for the duration, as usual.

The time is 10.30am when, after the breakfast chat shows, TV ratings struggle to maintain an audience.

But today might be one for the ratings record books, as Judge Kidd will etch into the Catholic Church's 2,000-year chequered history – in which, like a Hollywood western, evil has often tangled with good – what will be a new milestone in that story. In a 75-minute recitation, one lone, brave judge will take George Pell back to the day he allegedly committed one of the worst crimes imaginable, when the allegation is he used and abused children for his own satisfaction – in "God's house".

The judge is wearing purple.

Purple is customarily worn during the period of Lent when, in the weeks before Easter, it denotes suffering and sorrow and foretells the coming fate of the carpenter's son who became the *King of Kings* in death.

But purple is also the colour of justice and, worn by the judge in George Pell's trial on this auspicious day, it is a reminder of a distinguished career that has seen him on the world stage piecing together the facts that lead to justice for citizens who had suffered unimaginable war crimes of genocide and rape, often while many with the power to stop it were exercising their blindness, asleep at the wheel.

Judge Peter Kidd is a man of great courage. The war crimes of Bosnia-Herzegovina he once presided over might be in the past, but the memories of such judgements are none too distant on this day.

Kidd had sentenced the killers of Sergeant Gary Silk and Senior Constable Rodney Miller to life for which he was awarded Victoria Police's Medal of Commendation, the only recipient outside the force to do so.

Justice Peter Kidd is a singular man.

'A model of fairness and common sense,' says one of his peers.

The *New Daily's* website says its correspondent had been in the courtroom for all four days.

"We were all absolutely blown away by him…he is a credit to the justice system; he knew the case inside and out," says its correspondent, Lucie Morris-Marr.

"No man is an island," John Donne wrote. In one hour and a quarter, true justice will seemingly be served today upon a man who once thought he was safe.

Too big to fall.

"Never send for whom the bell tolls: it tolls for thee," Reverend John Donne, the parson-poet continued and today it rhymes.

The bells are ringing for George Pell.

<>

("Warning: contains details that may distress some readers", says the published transcript of Justice Peter Kidd's 75-minute sentencing speech):

"You pushed J's mouth onto your penis…"

"…you told (him) to take off his pants…"

"At some point you told (the frightened boys) to be quiet."

"Because they were crying…"

"'R' said to you: 'Can't you let us go? We didn't do anything…'"

"One month later…you pushed yourself against 'J.'"

(Pushed him) up against a wall…squeezing his genitals."

<>

Cardinal Pell is sentenced to "six years imprisonment (including) a non-parole period of three years and eight months."

He has been convicted on all five counts of abusing two choirboys, one of whom didn't live to see justice.

<>

"Forty-two months!"

"When I got life!"

"I'm serving a *life sentence*, after what happened to me."

"The judge should have thrown away the key."

"Money talks."

"Hadn't Richter confirmed Pell's guilt?"

"When he said those terrible, incriminating things."

"George Pell deserves to die in jail."

Victims are fuming. Collectively enraged by the sentence, which could have been for up to 14 years, most had experience and stories to tell about George Pell's cover-ups of crimes committed by Catholic Church members against their children.

Rage, rage against the fading of the light, cried poet, Dylan Thomas.

So, it goes on.

<>

The friend of Pell's accuser will never be forgotten; the grieving, angry father had been there in the court on all four days; he had followed every word in support of his son's brave friend.

Louise Milligan was a rare observer from the media on "judgement day" and describes the father's gruelling experience: "There was another victim of course, but he became a heroin addict at 14, a year after this crime and was an addict for the rest of his life until he died of an overdose at 30. His mother wept today."

The author of *Cardinal: The Rise and Fall of George Pell,* says of the accused's appearance: "His face was impassive...he continued to stare ahead; face as impervious as an Easter Island statue."

Months earlier, the journalist had endured six-and-a-half hours herself when she was grilled by Robert Richter QC at the original committal hearing, during which Pell's accuser had also been compelled to answer questions. It could never be said that Pell's impressive legal team hadn't been across the arguments from both sides.

And what of that brave young man, Pell's victim, who may never be identified?

Witness J is speaking through his lawyer: 'I appreciate that the court has acknowledged what was inflicted upon me as a child. But there can be no rest for me.'

<>

No rest for thousands, and while a throng of survivors of abuse has been standing in silent vigil outside the Melbourne Cathedral throughout the trial, another small group walks past.

Undeterred by events, they are intent on attending the regular 1 o'clock Mass; heads bowed, they avert their eyes.

Cardinal Pell has lived the 'life of Riley', often at home in the palace he had built in Rome, he was feted by the Church and his followers, both in Australia and the Vatican, for over two decades. All the while he had been an alleged child molester and protector of men who had been free to treat children as their macabre playthings, sexually abusing them, secure and trusted in their work as priests and other clerics in Catholic Orders.

Some years ago, many of us had wondered why Pell had shown such a poor choice of friends when he walked into a court arm-in-arm with that time's most notorious and serial child-sex fiend, Father Gerald Ridsdale.

One day soon, Gerald Ridsdale will make the headlines again, charged with 24 counts of raping four more young boys. A small mercy for these new victims will be that this priest will have already been jailed by then for the rest of his natural life.

Pell had hoodwinked three popes; and the name "George Pell" has been taken down from where it was once proudly displayed in his old stamping ground of Ballarat.

He has lost various patronages, including that of the place where he learnt his infamous "shirtfronting" tactic (see Father Michael Kelly's revealing essay in this book's Appendices), his once-cherished Richmond Football Club.

"The most dangerous place for a child was a Catholic Church," Chrissie Foster writes in Still Standing.

But visitors to the crypt of St Mary's, Sydney, noted for its exquisite mosaic floor in the style of a Celtic cross and that houses the tombs of the cathedral's previous archbishops, will discover today that of the eight sandstone sarcophagi there, one states:

"Cardinal George Pell 1941–2023"

<>

Even though Pell is off to prison, the whole saga will remain controversial.

Father Mick has softened his tune. 'George Pell is too smart to be so crazy.'

He is drawn into silence when I remind him the law of the land – 'twelve and true, accepted the evidence that he had (allegedly) raped those boys'.

And so it goes: I am astonished by the comment of Jesuit intellectual, Father Frank Brennan.

Brennan is much admired and will have carried many along with him – inviting controversy from others of us – when he stated that 'I hope a miscarriage of justice hasn't taken place today.'

I find both priests are discounting the veracity and courage of the young man under the microscope, known to the world forevermore, as *Witness J*.

<>

Pell appealed his convictions through the Victorian Court of Appeal and later through the High Court of Australia.

His appeal was upheld by the High Court, and he was freed from prison on 7 April 2020. The court found that the jury, acting reasonably, ought to have entertained a reasonable doubt regarding his guilt based on the evidence, which included timing inconsistencies that were not challenged by the prosecution.

<><>

2020
Set Free

Pell won on a legal technicality, according to Professor Ben Matthews and barrister Mark Thomas writing in the academic news outlet, *The Conversation:* the result is "An extraordinary outcome… The High Court decision may undermine confidence in the legal system, especially in child sexual abuse prosecutions."

Author David Marr explains it in *The Guardian:* "From the start the decision was simple: who was to be believed here, the young man who said he was raped after mass in the sacristy of St Patrick's Cathedral, or the church witnesses assembled by Pell's legal team – who claimed it wasn't possible?"

"The police, the prosecution authorities in Victoria, and two judges of the Court of Appeal in Melbourne believed the young man. They realised it was hard for Pell to rape that boy, but it was possible.

"The High Court has said *yes, possible, but not reasonably possible…* The judges do not accuse the young man of being a liar or a fantasist. They do not find his evidence contained discrepancies or displayed inadequacies 'of such a character as to require the jury to have entertained a doubt as to guilt'."

"But they have done what the jury and the Victorian Court of Appeal did not do: they have trusted absolutely the evidence of Pell's master of ceremonies, Monsignor Charles Portelli."

"This church official said he had always been with the archbishop that morning, first on the steps of the cathedral farewelling the faithful, and then in the sacristy helping him unrobe."

"The High Court observed that Portelli's evidence of having an actual recall of being with Pell on the steps was never challenged by the prosecution."

"Believe Portelli here and it is hard to believe the man who accuses Pell of rape."

The man who accused George Pell of rape – I am struck with the horror of those words: the horror that, after all Witness J has been through – knowing, as I was once told, that the memory of being raped cannot be forgotten – *rape is the murder of the soul.*

"Doubt": it has a way of playing with our minds and I find I'm not alone with it.

The New York Times: "There were other allegations that were no part of the case. In February 2019 a second trial, in which Cardinal Pell was accused of touching boys in a swimming pool was cancelled because of legal setbacks."

"Karen Monument, the sister of one of the men in that case, said her brother and the family were 'devastated' that Cardinal Pell would now walk free."

"Phil Nagle, an advocate for abuse survivors from Ballarat, Cardinal Pell's hometown, said that he and others were shocked by the judgement, which engendered further distrust of a court system that has failed to bring many abusers to justice."

<>

Meanwhile, Chrissie Foster is a forlorn figure, caught by the camera with her head in her hands on the front steps of her small, brick home in inner Melbourne.

'I'm devastated. This is devastating,' says the mother of two beautiful girls, one dead by suicide, the other wheelchair-bound now and both victims of Catholic priest, Kevin O'Donnell, a man protected by Pell, and lauded at his funeral.

Before her husband Anthony's untimely death, Chrissie Foster had said she would never set foot in a Catholic Church again and had recently informed the Victorian Parliamentary Inquiry she was breaking the Church's confidentiality clause when she said Anthony's family was awarded $750,000. Chrissie said at the time she had hoped 'others will sue the Catholic Church for better compensation (that was marked by Pell's $50,000 ceiling)'.

This news has prompted *Broken Rites* to hope more victims will fight for true justice from the courts.

Ian Lawther says he hasn't prayed so much in his life, and he hopes the 'terrible disappointment' of the High Court decision will be short-lived. It couldn't possibly be over. Could it?

Not with the other alleged sex assaults upon children, or the alleged crimes covered up in support of terrible people, such as Pell's close priest friends, Ridsdale and O'Donnell.

Ironically, it falls on Easter Sunday 2020 for the editorial in the News Limited tabloid to explain the Pell decision succinctly:

"George Pell has not been declared 'innocent' and neither has the Catholic Church. It would be wise for the Church to remember this when it considers what to do next with its former leader. How the Church handles the High Court decision and Pell's freedom is as important as the reaction to the guilty verdict itself. If there is a genuine desire for healing – and everyone from the Pope down says there is – Pell cannot be simply ushered back into the fold."

<>

Freed from prison and hoping to live the quiet life in Rome, Cardinal George Pell was being interviewed on the BBC's *Heart and Soul* program.

Asked about his time in jail, he said: 'The worst single thing was the strip-searches.'

Lying in his prison bed, did he ever think about those two pubescent altar boys?

'Of course I did,' he said. 'One of them died years ago.'

"But I'm a pretty good sleeper."

<><>

2020
"A Strong Stomach"

"You'll need a strong stomach to digest *Revelation's* insights into child sexual abuse in the Catholic Church," writes The Guardian's Brigid Delaney.

George Pell's month-long wait for the High Court to make its decision had seen one of Australia's finest TV journalists, Sarah Ferguson, putting the final touches to a long, truth-telling exposé of the Catholic Church; the child-rape crimes that went unrecognised in their vast numbers by the Church, while the protection racket it had become was slowly destroying the institution from within.

Running to almost four hours, and aired on *ABC TV* over three nights in March, while George Pell was still in prison, *Revelation* joins the *Spotlight* film in exposing priests' and other clerics' crimes that the Vatican had ignored, dismissed and turned its blind eye to while children suffered in their hundreds, perhaps many thousands – dying in a drug-fuelled, inebriated stupor by suicide.

While the earlier American film had won the Academy Award for Best Picture, the Australian version is an epic masterpiece of television journalism that would claim awards of its own.

Sarah Ferguson needed a strong stomach when she "came face to face with two of the worst paedophiles".

"I'm used to intense projects, but this one has been more intense and more challenging than anything I have ever done," Sarah said in an interview with journalist, Natasha Johnson.

"Throughout the long-running scandal of clerical abuse in Australia there was one voice we hadn't heard and that was the perpetrators. I wanted to ask them how they led their double lives and how the Church enabled them."

"But how do you interview men whose crimes are so vile and disturbing, who've committed crimes against vulnerable children? It was a struggle not to let my revulsion at their crimes drag me off course."

<>

'I didn't know that what I was doing was wrong,' says priest Vincent Ryan, his face hauntingly impassive.

'I don't believe you,' says Sarah Ferguson.

'I do now,' he says. He says he is thankful for the Seal of Confession that always absolved him – Ferguson reminding him that, by doing so, he made the priests he chose to confess to complicit in his life of constant rape and abuse.

Ryan died in 2022. Despite multiple convictions for child sexual abuse, he remained a Catholic priest.

<>

Revelation is historiographic in its breadth: the tragedies revealed are Shakespearean; the series features complex "stars" of the Church.

One is long-time secretary of the Bishops' Conference, Brian Lucas.

Appearing on camera in his customary business suit, Father Brian Lucas is the bard's "devil in a pleasing shape" when he tells Ferguson he refuses to accept the responsibility he had for giving victims any promise of justice.

Looking deeply into the camera lens, his large, round face is opaque in his reply when, unmoved by the accusation, his black eyes set like marbles in stone, he attempts to convince the *Revelation* audience why it was 'under the rules!'. Lucas protests that the meetings he had with offending priests had to be carried out in secret.

'Or they (the priests) wouldn't have come to me in the first place,' he protests.

'You are speaking about the Seal of Confession.'

'No.'

'What then?'

Lucas says he prefers the word 'confidentiality'.

Father Brian Lucas could have used his power as General Secretary of the Australian Bishops Conference to help clean up the Church's sexual abuse problem. Instead, he had no mind for clerical crimes, nor the victims; it was always only ever the Church for him.

Among the worst offenders Lucas had protected came from the Order of *St John of God.*

The Order had a list of 31 names of paedophile priests in the Australian branch of *St John of God* alone. According to the Royal Commission, that's

40 per cent of the Order's priests.

They were defended by Father Brian Lucas.

<>

Of all the paedophile priests that walked the streets of Catholicism untouched for so long, none worse than George Pell's friend and his last cellmate, Gerald Ridsdale.

Revelation finds Ridsdale's sister.

Now of some great age, and sightless, the older sibling says her brother turned up at her home, unannounced one day, and they got talking.

'How many were there? Was it one, two?' asked the priest's sister.

The old woman says his answer has shamed her family forever and a day.

'He said it was "in the hundreds".'

'You mustn't be ashamed,' Ferguson says, in the soft, consoling voice she displays in times of empathy.

<>

"Shame": I have lived with that word for over three decades, and throughout the Ferguson interviews, they were bound to bring my own memories back.

They did so often as, seeing one victim after another telling his story, those times resurfaced through veils of tears.

"Steve" was too ashamed to give out his full name. He says he wants the church and presbytery where the priest had anally raped him demolished.

Now in his middle age, Steve's words must ring out in many such "holy" places across the world.

'It's a crime scene,' he says.

There's the amazing Audrey Nash, yet another mother of a son who suicided.

Once a daily Mass-goer, now grieving for her loss, Mrs Nash angrily adds to "Steve's" description of the Catholic Church as 'a criminal organisation' and she goes on to declare that the paedophilia where she lives in Ballarat was so rampant 'it had to be organised for them to get away with it for so long'.

Audrey Nash speaks of the days after her son's suicide.

'When three local clerics arrived at my door, I had assumed they had come to console me. But that was until they appeared particularly anxious to know if Andrew had said anything before his death. After that, they left me high and dry,' she says.

The one-time fervent Mass-goer has not had a visit from a priest, or any other Catholic cleric, since.

<>

Revelation introduces two more victims of alleged early abuse by George Pell: young boys, now middle-aged men, in a swimming pool in Ballarat.

They had earlier tried to take the case to trial, but the court ruled there was insufficient evidence.

Now appearing older than their years, they want the truth 'out there' and hope that telling their stories will see the Church 'listen'.

Like so many others, they want people to know what has been done to them in the name of God; the despair is writ large on their ravaged faces.

'My life has been broken.'

'Nobody believed me.'

<>

Revelation also speaks to a man who was once a boarder at St Alypius in Ballarat.

He had been asked by Big George to help with the weeding at the presbytery.

The new boy was still finding his feet in the boarding school and was trusting of those in charge, or his parents wouldn't have placed him at St Alypius where he would get the good education that would have him ready for the world.

He wasn't prepared to grow up suddenly, as he did that day when 'thrown to the lions' in the shape of one of the priests.

He thought he knew 'Father George' well, being an altar boy; but he certainly got more than expected, when, job done, it was suggested he had a shower.

'You can't go home like that, look at you, you're filthy,' he told *Broken Rites*.

He says Pell soon joined him in the shower where 'he said he'd show me how to soap myself'.

As if the confused youngster didn't know.

'Soon I was being washed everywhere imaginable, and he was getting me to soap him too.'

And then?

'He was behind me, and I felt his penis pressing against me. I turned and looked, got dressed quickly and fled. I will never forget that.'

'What happened next?'

'I was sitting outside in the garden when George Pell offered me a lift home.'

Wise to accept, the young boy's home being 'miles away', the priest he would soon learn went under the moniker "Big George" gave his scared victim a dollar.

'A brown note, it was. Pell told me not to say anything to anyone about what had taken place. I didn't tell the sisters – nuns – or anyone. But who would believe a little boy?" he says, grieving with the memory of a long-ago nightmare that has come back to haunt him – as it often did.

His hope is that others who share his pain might come forward with their own story.

'Take the shame you brought on me, Cardinal Pell. Here, take it,' he says suddenly in Ferguson's *Revelation*.

He starts up the motorbike he has been leaning against and is seen sweeping round the lonely country roads where he now lives.

A small farm, thanks to the reasonable court-awarded compensation he fought for and that has given him a new life, with prized horses to help block out the dark days he wished would stay behind him.

They're not over yet, but talking about it helps in the pushback.

Many such men who were once frightened boys took their own lives or went on to live lonely lives with no mercy from the main perpetrator of the crimes done against them: the Catholic Church.

<><>

2023
Sole Survivor

May is the autumn of Pope Francis' Commission for the Protection of Minors – the pope's initiative 'to repair the damage done by previous generations and to those who continue to suffer. This is the moment of reparation,' he says upon announcing the members to 'face one of the greatest challenges of our time.'

The pope is demanding that every diocese is to 'set aside places for receiving accusations and caring for those who report that they have been harmed'.

'You are the light of the world,' the pope says, and that responsibility has become a 'universal law of the Catholic Church'. *Vos Estis Lux Mundi.*

'No one today can honestly claim to be unaffected by the reality of sexual abuse in the Church.'

Francis quotes American activist and poet Maya Angelou, who said: "I've learned that people will forget what you said, people will forget what you did, but people will never forget how you made them feel."

They're fine words: 'The pope talks a good talk,' said a disenchanted victim when the pope, shaped as poor peasant Jorge Bergoglio, first grappled with the poison chalice he had been handed by the failing Pope Benedict XVI.

Many lapsed Catholics that I know are speaking of the Church's "own goal": 'Can't you hear the marching feet?' says Nick, quoting *Les Misérables.*

Is revolution nigh?

A new Reformation?

Reality bites, and it is only sixty or so years since German priest Joseph Ratzinger declared the Catholic Church was always destined to shrink.

But, as Pope Benedict, he fled responsibilities, leaving the pope we call "remarkable" with the impossible task he has set himself – of returning the Catholic Church to where it has always belonged – in the hands of *the people of God.*

<><><>

Six

BETRAYAL: IT'S PERSONAL

2023
Death of Pell

'They bumped him off.'

January 11th, the day after George Pell died in Rome, will be hot and sticky for the one-day cricket at the SCG. Father Mick is on the phone.

'Would have been easy.'

'To stick a needle in his bum.'

He says: 'They had been waiting for the moment.'

To rid the Catholic Church of George Pell.

Mick had long been disgusted by the backlash against the 1960 reforms that had culminated in the arrival of John Paul II and Benedict XVI, with both papacies clinging to "papal infallibility". Father Mick retired from the institutional Church at 65. Mick has recently turned 90 and has been working for the people of God on his own terms all these years, hoping he'll be alive to see the dream for the Church he shares with the pope he calls "Frankie" find fruition in the real Catholic Church.

'You sure about that, Mick?' I asked him.

The news from the Vatican is that Pell's sudden death was due to "heart complications from hip surgery".

'A toxic needle in the bum,' Mick repeats, reprising the possible way Pope John XX111's successor, John Paul I died. An innocent man had passed on that day.

<>

The death of Pell has fired up the commentariat:

A new Cathy Wilcox cartoon of a tombstone in an otherwise empty graveyard.

Meanwhile, the father of the altar boy who committed suicide is saying through his solicitor that he is continuing the civil claim he had brought against both Cardinal Pell and the Catholic Church.

"There is still a great deal of evidence for this claim to rely on," Lisa Flynn, an expert in Catholic Church crimes, informs *The New Daily*.

The claimant "had suffered psychological injury…and his earning capacity was diminished", Flynn says.

While an earlier judge had dismissed the Church's attempt to have the father's case against George Pell and the Catholic Church disallowed (Pell's defence being that the father was not "a direct victim"), we are told the trial will go ahead "on the grounds it is in the public interest".

His death "hasn't changed public opinions of Cardinal Pell – a divisive figure until the end," Flynn says.

But it seems opinion is divided on that: on February 2 of 2023, they had to close the streets around Sydney's St Mary's Cathedral for Pell's funeral.

The body had been lying "in state" in the cathedral's stone-cold interior ever since its arrival from Rome three days earlier. While victims had been appalled by the veneration, some recalled the *Godfather* film – a quick look at the sarcophagus to make sure he was dead.

The day of the requiem Mass saw a packed church.

Mantillas, newly bought, stood out like veiled disguises and sweet incense drifted over the attendees' heads. Many in the crowd had already started tearing up when that most flamboyant of archbishops, Anthony Fisher, began the solemn High Mass – he most assuredly owed the man who had once installed him as his successor in the coveted Sydney cathedral.

Later, it will be said that Pell's solemn funeral had been saved by the music. But for his alleged victims, there won't be any peace. The Pell chapter will never be closed for them.

<>

The Sydney Morning Herald of January 14 is bristling with stories on George Pell.

Chip Le Grand's **Shadow of a Giant** covers three pages of broadsheet, beginning with:

"Tony Abbott once described Pell's incarceration as a form of crucifixion and declared him a saint for our times."

Chrissie Foster tempers her response, but her grief at the statement is palpable:

'Anyone seeking to canonise Pell should read the findings of the Royal Commission into Child Sex Abuse in his time in the Ballarat and Melbourne dioceses.'

'Any consideration of making new saints by the Catholic Church should be reserved for the many victims of priests who suicided under Pell's watch.'

<>

I seek Ian Lawther's reaction to the titan's death.

How does he feel, now your nemesis has left the planet?'

'Relief,' Ian says. 'Thank God it's over. I've been harbouring this moment for 30 years.'

'The Church has been set free to grow,' he tells me.

He remembers a phone call he once had from George Pell: 'It was in response to my efforts to get the Church to be forthright in accepting its responsibilities.'

'"George Pell here, Ian," he said. '"What do you want?"'

Ian Lawther told the man who would be cardinal that he wanted the Church to accept its responsibilities – and 'fess up'.

'I was demanding the Catholic Church recognise the serial abuse that has been going on for years.'

What did Pell say to that?

'There's nothing wrong with my Church, Ian.'

Ian Lawther hadn't heard from the cardinal since.

<>

The death of Pell prompts some to revisit the out-of-touch hierarch's idea of "Church".

Catholic historian and one-time priest, Paul Collins, writes of Pell's preference for a "fortress Catholicism…a triumphalist Church in which there is no room for compromise".

The author of *Mixed Blessings* says he still remembers Pell on ABC TV, "saying that Christ established a priesthood at the Last Supper".

"A ridiculous notion," Collins scoffs. "As though Jesus set up seminaries to train clergymen in the modern sense."

The Catholic historian claims that when he challenged this, "Pell scorned the idea. For him, the priesthood was of divine origin and unchanging."

He says, "I had become convinced that Catholicism had to continue applying the reforms begun by the Second Vatican Council (1962–65)."

Collins recognises the ongoing Francis reforms as a lasting monument to the far-seeing revolutionary Pope John XXIII (who he believes saved the Church).

"Vatican II developed a dynamic understanding of Catholicism that was opening up to the contemporary world and even learning from it.

"'Throwing open the windows', in a poetic sense, as the pope had said at the time (of the Vatican Council)."

George Pell had been intent on closing them.

But Collins says, "Pell's absolutist Catholicism was fast fading (before his death). Pell's stance on an infallible pope only applied when it was a pope who agreed with him."

Pell, the betrayer. It was as personal as the story of Judas and his friend, Jesus.

But, unlike the apostle who betrayed Jesus Christ, did "the man who got off" – despite Australia's highest court failing to declare George Pell innocent – ever come to *feel his guilt?*

<>

Recently, I have learnt that Brother Ross Murrin — who had been my youngest son's Year 7 Dorm Master — had once written to the Marist Leader, who had once been one of his protectors, seeking his help in getting Murrin out of the North Queensland jail.

Although most would say that Murrin's multiple crimes are not a reason for clemency, and the prisoner's lamenting that 'life is hard in jail… (he felt) he had done his time' … would resonate with very few people, his protests ought to fall upon deaf ears.

He and his supporters in the Church were to soldier on, and early 2024 saw a judge sympathetic to the paedophile's plea, release Ross Murrin on the grounds that his 94-year-old father required his looking after.

Hearing the news, the cry came: "That judge should have thrown away the key!"

Adding salt to the wound, the court heard Murrin's multiple child rapes described as "indiscretions".

They were not.

They were crimes.

The Church authorities had moved "the murderer of children's souls" from school to school to school – *eleven* times.

In the Catholic world of those times, there were always more children for their clerics so inclined to feast upon.)

<>

The institutional Church has lost me, and I still carry the memory of that line of dormant bushes that lined the path to the Marist leader's door, and the betrayals of what turned out to be more children every single day that has inspired this book.

Those roses were in bud then but would soon be telling lies to anyone eager to smell their exquisite fragrance – unaware often of what was ahead when they would grasp the thorny stems.

I had run away from the Marist leader's request in dismay and astonishment that day, but not Jesus, who I found again in Sicily one day when I was chasing an interest in the Mafia Trials – inspired by Peter Robb's extraordinary account of murder and political corruption, "Midnight in Sicily" - and came across the Church that inspired me to change my life.

And steered me on a new course.

<><>

2023
One Fine Day

'I wish we had known that Brother Stephen was buggering our classmates,' Nick had said of his time in the 1950s when he boarded at the school he still calls "Joey's".

'It wasn't until the turn of the millennium. And that's forty years,' he says, regretting the pain those boys must have carried.

We have just learnt that an unprecedented event recently took place at the school

The latest news has been in all the newspapers; and it's not pretty: there's a photograph taken just inside the forbidding iron gates that had been transferred from Sydney Town Hall over a century ago in 1881.

Recently, a small group of survivors of sexual abuse at the hands of some of the Marist Brothers who taught at the elite boarding school were joined by the current headmaster and other sympathisers in the inauguration of a memorial to the horrors that had taken place there right up to the 1990s.

They learn the Marist leadership had received 128 complaints of child sexual abuse in one 10-year period alone. The Sydney province had a little over 200 members at the time.

A survivor spoke: 'We're standing here in front of a multimillion-dollar aquatic facility, so it's perhaps surprising that this memorial was funded by donations,' said Andrew Phelan, who had left the college in 1971 and had been one of the installation's initiators. The hope is there will be many more such ex-pupils, some with deep pockets; and not all having suffered as Andrew had.

'One way of looking at this memorial is it's a gift from victims and survivors, their friends and supporters,' he said.

'There's nothing that cannot be talked about, and sex abuse is no longer a secret.'

Nor is it a shame for victims and their families.

<>

November in Sydney is a contrary month that, despite summer coming on, embraces the seasons. Bring an umbrella in case.

But today has turned out to be fine and warm with wispy clouds and the occasional jet trail streaking across the sky. It is the Spring Fair at Joey's, and I am waiting for Nick to join me at the memorial. No names, but it recognises the terrible roll call of boys who had been sexually abused by Marist Brothers while their masters had looked away.

It was Nick's idea to check the memory out.

'You heard?' he had said.

Yes.'

'Well, we had better go and see it. Hadn't we?'

Nick has picked the Spring Fair because we'd be lost in the crowd, I guess. He is hoping the Museum of Champions will be open. Nick wants to see what has changed. He said there have been reports 'that the buggers had tinkered with the team photos'.

I have been here a while; it is just me and the memorial. I am alone with my thoughts in sad contemplation, waiting.

Built of Sydney sandstone to reflect the original grand Victorian building, the memorial stands – or rather, squats, it being low to the ground and broad of beam – inside the school's entrance, those massive and somewhat forbidding iron gates.

The brand-new structure is spherical in shape and on a slant; about four feet off the ground at its highest point, it's out of whack on a tilt, and the smooth sandstone falls away to a small round pool.

Nick has arrived and we share our immediate reaction: that the structure reflects victims sliding into the water in a symbol of drowning in their pain.

While people continue to enter the college grounds, most avert their eyes and are as dismissive of us as they are of this new symbol of "college".

The terrible crimes that once plagued its hallowed halls.

It is a pause for thought.

<>

I have discovered something amiss.

'Read the plaque,' I say.

"This memorial is dedicated to those who were victims of abuse while students at the College."

'Notice anything missing?'

Nick is instantly startled by the realisation that it is the word *"sexual"*.

'We're talking about *sexual* abuse,' he says.

'There is no mention anywhere on this memorial of the sexual abuse so many boys were subject to here.'

 'Over so many years. At St Joseph's College, Hunter's Hill.'

Where Nick, his brother, and – I am perishing the thought – *my four sons!* – went to school.

Like so many instances of half-hearted attempts to recognise the Catholic Church had once housed monsters, the memorial is disingenuous. To future generations, it will speak of a violent place where kids were bashed up, but their souls left intact, life had gone on.

The Catholic Church has always been good at burying the worst of its truths.

'Typical!' cries Nick.

Nick wants to check out Joey's famous sporting heritage that is housed within the main building.

Memories of the champion teams, we soon have that prized collection of photos to ourselves.

Nick homes in on photos from his time at college and looks at them keenly, one by one.

'Brother Stephen should be among them, he was a rugby coach,' he says.

Finding where he should be, square in the centre of his champion team, we turn away in disgust at the blotted-out face among those strapping young athletes.

Faceless Stephen is not alone. All the known child molesters have been deliberately disfigured, their faces made unrecognisable by modern pixelation.

It's sad for victims who want the truth exposed: that the esteemed college's long line of successful First Fifteen rugby teams, which included a string of ten in the 1950s, has been blurred by coaches who preyed upon their muscular charges with rubdowns that went further and by master tacticians who knew how to use their power.

Only the boys' names are mentioned, with their offending coaches in disguise.

"NAME WITHHELD".

Nick finds the winning athletic team from his final year, points to a robust young man, and tells me with tears welling up, that he has heard recently the news that the boy who had once brought glory to "Joey's" had 'committed suicide'.

We leave now and, having had such horrors to ourselves, we make our way through a smaller crowd than either of us remembers for the Spring Fair.

We are sad and angry that what happened here had been covered up for so long.

Such is shame.

As we take our leave of that place of good and bad memories, Nick has gone quiet.

We grab coffee up the road, when my friend says suddenly: 'You've got the end of your book.'

We exchange rueful smiles.

<>

Now it is two years later, and Nick is informing me he had been at a school reunion, when one of his classmates, who was in the First Fifteen forwards of Brother Stephen's team had confirmed to him the coach would sometimes give 'intimate' massages after training, whereupon he would get 'all the boys to strip off and enjoy hosing them down with a fire hose'.

The story would be new to many; but such is power when it is in the hands of a lone ranger who has been made so by the exalted position he had been handed by his chiefs.

<><>

2025
Compensation for victims of Father George Pell

"The True Legacy Of The Rapist George Pell" was the cover story of February's *The Monthly.*

Award-winning journalist, Louise Milligan's incisive review had been withheld from publication in February 2025 in the interests of a parallel legal case, but it was published following settlement in the case.

The news that George Pell is alleged to have already been abusing young boys when the church placed its newly minted priest in the paedophile hunting ground of 1970s Ballarat is staggering.

But the ghost of Cardinal Pell has failed to hide from civil justice, after two men were awarded compensation under the Australian Government's National Redress Scheme. One of the boys allegedly raped by Pell at Ballarat in a school gymnasium, when he was nine, while the other was groped during a game at a swimming pool, aged eight. The year 3 student (at the time) says Pell grabbed his genitals while throwing him up in the air.

Michael James, the former of the two boys, says 'Pell raped him, after chasing him over a stolen cardigan.'

"The victims attended different schools and did not know each other," Milligan writes.

"James remembers Pell saying, 'Pull your pants down. He pulled out his belt and I thought he was going to whip me. He didn't.'"

"Instead, James recounted how Pell anally raped him. 'It was very painful. I was bleeding from my bottom afterward.'

Five decades passed before James informed his mother, Carmel, of the rape.

"'I was tortured by the fact that, for 50 years, my son lived alone with that horror,' she says.

"The Redress Scheme's decision maker said that other victims from his school had also accused Pell of abuse."

Meanwhile, the wife of the other boy (who prefers to be unnamed) expressed frustration over the Catholic Church's continued reverence for Pell. "It is very hard to see the church provide so much pomp and ceremony around Pell's absurd funeral," she said.

While criminal cases, as in Pell's, require proof "beyond reasonable doubt"- a bar that proved to be too high for the High Court - the National Redress Scheme operates on the basis of "reasonable likelihood".

<>< ><>

Seven
THE NEW CHURCH

2013
Two Very Different Popes

After the upheaval brought on by the 1960's changes due to Vatican II, and the battle between old Church conservatives and Pope John XXIII's reforming zeal, a brave young priest of that time presented his radical ideas to a German radio audience.

Joseph Ratzinger had just turned 40 in 1969 when he said: 'From today's crisis, a Church will emerge tomorrow that will have lost a great deal. She will be small and to a large extent will have to start from the beginning. She will no longer be able to fill many of the buildings created in her period of great splendour. Because of the smaller number of her followers, she will lose many of her privileges in society.'

Thirty-six years later, Joseph telegraphed what sort of pope he would be as Benedict XVI, channelling a 5th-century saint who put education at the forefront of learning, as well as trust in God's miracles.

Benedict's reign lasted eight years and his resignation in 2013 was the first in 600 years; the heralding in of the Francis papacy was to bring grief to the hard-liners who had once tamed the pope, and the German's death in 2021 solved the *Two Popes* problem that had plagued the first years of Francis' pontificate.

St Francis is known as "the champion of the poor" and yet, his dealings with the Argentinian Generals had many thinking Jorge Bergoglio might be needing some of his papal namesake's "miracles" to survive – especially with the "priests' problem" Benedict had tossed him (brought to the fore last year when the Vatican released a letter from Benedict asking for forgiveness over his failure to act on *paedophile* crimes by priests while he was archbishop of Munich).

But his Jesuit successor is a humble man and politically astute: Austin Ivereigh says in the *Wounded Shepherd* that while the new pope's circling enemies in the curia had immediately homed in on Bergoglio's generous dealings with the murderous Videla regime, in truth his placating of the tyrant had allowed him to save many of his fellow countrymen by hiding them in the bishopric and swimming them across the river into Uruguay in the dead of night.

Ivereigh writes that "hundreds, some say thousands" of Argentinians avoided being tortured and shot for their socialist beliefs due to Bergoglio.

If anyone could change the Church forever, the resolute but softly spoken South American Pope Francis could.

Upon his election, the new pope was instantly recognised to be "a man of the people" when he chose to dress plainly like a humble priest; there'd be no Gucci red slippers for this occupant of the Holy See's highest office, the new pope chose to wear the workaday shoes of his countrymen.

But it was his choice not to live in the pope's palace, choosing a small cottage in the Vatican grounds instead, that turned heads among the cardinals, many of whom saw themselves as "princes of the realm".

Where were they expected to meet their pope if not in regal splendour?

Undeterred, Francis went on to swap the Mercedes for a less ostentatious family vehicle, the popular Ford Focus.

Pope Francis displays none of Mencken's description of a bishop as "a Christian ecclesiastic of a rank superior to that of Christ".

He would follow his Jesuit vows of poverty and chastity and sees himself as a *poverello* – "little poor man" – hoping to mirror Christ in simplicity and love.

Francis stories soon abounded. His first act as pope was to wash the feet of 12 young prisoners: Muslims, Jews and Christians, all sorts, both men and women, and his kindness and empathy blossomed.

Ivereigh writes of a story that the pope was once seen moving among the faithful in St Peter's Square when a group of pilgrims called out to him: 'Jorge, Jorge, come over here.'

Apparently, the pope jumped down from the safety of the papal cart against all protocol and excitedly embraced the people one by one.

Upon his return, he was gently castigated by his security head who had been assuming the worst.

'But I wasn't in any danger,' Francis protested. Didn't they understand? 'These people are Argentinians; they are not cardinals!'

And what would the pope say to a gay priest? The question once asked by a cheeky reporter, only to be surprised by the answer.

'Who am I to judge?' he said, in a sign that the Vatican is under new management. Contrary to Benedict's hope that a "small church" would return to conservatism, the church renewed itself; medievalism is behind it, and the "people of God" are rising to the top.

<><>

2019
Sicily's Mikvah

'I love it, I love it – *I love it!*' he cries with excited eyes.

His T-shirt flutters and comes to rest against his lean, bony torso; it is worn hung out in the current fashion of the young (and those who wish to appear so), with cheap blue jeans for a companion. He could have been a university student or advertising creative; he isn't though.

'I'm the parish priest!' he exclaims delightedly, as if it is all he ever wanted to be.

But there's more, much more and we will soon be amazed when the Church – his beloved *"chiesa"* – reveals itself through its chirpy keeper who can't believe his luck today with four Australian Catholics who had been showing interest in his small ancient stone church.

<>

We – us: being cheaper to travel in numbers, my wife, Helen and I, along with two female friends of long-standing acquaintance, had been in surprising Syracuse for almost a week when we came upon the 18th-century Catholic church of Saint Phillip the Apostle. It has crossed our paths in the best way possible: by accident on our wanderings through streets so narrow we often must press ourselves against the walls to allow a rare vehicle to pass.

Few cars are permitted in Syracuse's old city. It was the place to stay in solid, greying apartment buildings, some of which go back to medieval times when barbarism was always just below the surface. The city's most fabled tale is of a rich Italian Count who, after informing his long-time mistress that he was returning to his wife, had his head cut off while sleeping. The story goes that his jilted paramour had placed the severed head on her balcony where she "would have her lover forever". Colourful porcelain heads in various sizes from very small to life-size abound everywhere in this mediaeval stronghold. Denied the latter, a stunningly handsome creation, on practical grounds, I was placated with a pair of salt and pepper shakers.

We've been on the road a month by now and are "churched-out" – we'd had enough of *cathedrals* anyway. "Museums of the future", the way the Catholic Church is going. Wouldn't the moral thing – let's be frank about this: the *Christian* thing – have been to look after the poor first?

While the Church amassed a fortune in art, didn't it take its eye off the hungry? (One-time priest, Morris West's best-selling '60s' novel, *The Shoes of the Fisherman*, concludes with a tortured pope selling it all up in a Marxian act that is both a metaphorical allegory and real.)

"It is easier for a camel to go through the eye of a needle than for a rich man to enter the kingdom of God." (Matthew 19:24)

Still, the cathedral-hunters come off the buses. Follow your guide, the one holding a flag, fill the massive sacred edifices with noise and shuffling, one after another, and gaze in wonder and amazement; and awe at how it was done! But...

How many people died building this?

Watch the curious, the reverent and otherwise, wandering these museums that could house millions of refugees.

<>

Ironically, the young priest's name is Phillip, named after the 1st-century CE apostle who had converted the legendary Palestinian magician known as the "Magus", and reared four daughters, all of whom are seen to be prophets.

He informs us that the *Chiesa di San Filippo Apostolo* is his first parish, and he has turned out to be a veritable chatterbox who says he is pleased we aren't a large number, preferring personal engagement rather than to take on a crowd.

But, while the more compelling 7th-century Duomo that dominates the main piazza claims to have its roots in a pagan temple to the Greek goddess of Athena, the story of Saint Phillip the Apostle also has the honour of embracing both books of the Bible and is as much Moses and Jeremiah as Jesus and Mary.

The Chiesa is not ornate. Its only tilt to grandness is Corinthian columns, one to either side of a heavy wooden door, above which is a simple balcony where we can imagine early priests spoke to the overflow crowd; and above the balcony an heraldic shield that represents the apostle from Bethsaida who had joined Jesus before going on to preach in Greece and Syria, where some say he died of natural causes. Although other Church historians prefer a tale that has St Phillip sharing the same fate as Jesus (the mythology often more powerful than the fact in the Catholic Church).

The truth about "our" – we have claimed this wondrous place already – simple 300-year-old church is another reason why we have chosen it over the more opulent grand *Duomo*. We learn beloved *St Filippo* was erected by the local community, and with a rich multicultural history grounded in Greek, Roman, Arab and Jewish culture.

The Jews' story in Syracuse was one of protection followed by persecution that forced the people to depart in the year of Columbus, 1492. Although, three centuries later the enlightened Neapolitan Governor, Charles III invited the Jews back, few accepted, and by 1742 a Christian church was being built above their legendary synagogue.

<>

Our interest peaked by Father Phillip's interesting narrative, we haven't moved beyond the entrance (we are not allowed into the simple body of the church that is undergoing renovation and unsafe). We are eager for more, but there is an interruption, one that will soon enthral our hearts.

A young woman has arrived; dark in complexion and with a serious air, she is an instant curiosity. A brief conversation with the priest reveals she is from Tel Aviv, where she has been living for the past six years. Originally from the Czech Republic, she is in Syracuse for a school friend's wedding. Although she appears distant and quiet, Phillip's impish delight at her sudden appearance has increased tenfold.

'I love this place!' he bursts out once more in what has become his customary way and for the first time apologises for his broken English, presenting us with a brief smile when we confess to our rudimentary Italian.

'I hope you are ready to be surprised,' he says, urging us to a small window set in the stone floor. 'This is why I love Chiesa Filippo so much,' he says.

'Look,' he cries, switching on lights and we are entranced, gazing at a deep shaft that appears at first to go into the centre of the Earth, an ancient well.

'Come. Come,' he says invitingly, and turns to us with an intriguing smile. 'You didn't know about our *mikvah?*'

'No,' I reply, remembering stories about the Jews' sacred baths.

Hundreds of tiny lights sparkle in the still, bluish waters and we can already feel our hearts pumping when our Israeli companion stifles a strange, eerie cry at the sight of the holy waters that has stirred all our souls forevermore.

I am moved to recall James A. Michener's *The Source*, that follows a spring seeping from a crack in the rockface of an otherwise barren land.

"Where there is water, there is life," is the central message of Michener's historical novel, that expands upon the theme and chronicles the history of the Jews who built their villages wherever water was found.

'Come,' says the young priest.

We are told we will be gone a while, but that's no matter. We have time and are already wishing for this new adventure to go on and on.

Steep stone steps lead us down a rough-hewn passage, the jagged bits smoothed over; carved out by hand with limited tools way back when construction must have taken an inordinate time but would have been one of excitement – and in this sacred place, love of God.

We are on the first lower floor – he has warned us it is a very long way down – and with three floors to go, we are informed we are in what had once been a Christian burial chamber for wealthy locals.

'There were bones here,' the excited *padre* Phillip says ambiguously. They are empty now, all of that is memory, including faint frescoes depicting the Stations of the Cross; but why were the bodies taken away?

'Oh, there was much to do,' our host tells us matter-of-factly of the recent renovation.

We continue to make our way down gingerly in the feeble light given by concealed globes that appear strategically at four or five-pace intervals; on sensors, they switch off, leaving pitch darkness behind us as new ones light up ahead.

Saving electricity, an illusion of shadows morphs into gentle illumination, the fading light eerily drifting in and out in front and behind.

The next floor is a revelation: one of a series of tunnels that we are hastily informed was once a network that runs everywhere beneath the island of Ortigia (old Syracuse) and to the sea. Apparently, 2,000 years ago the Greeks had built much of the tunnel system to conduit the town's water.

But we soon learn, it became one of the few places of safety when during the Italian war Mussolini had established a garrison in Syracuse, and with the Allies bombarding the island, the tunnels were ready-made bomb shelters. Our guide pointed out faint images of British planes and a parachute on a wall.

'My parents were here. Sometimes 10,000 people lived in this place,' Phillip explains mournfully. 'They were often here for days, weeks.'

But that is in the past and he makes a down gesture. More steps, Jewish steps that are smoother. These stone masons had been meticulous.

"Work is love made visible," I recall the Lebanese prophet Khalil Gibran had written in his book; these days *The Prophet* is often first cab off the rank in secular weddings.

'The Jews made all these steps,' Phillip says, obviously proud of their work.

His excitement has reached boiling point.

And here it is, the subdued lighting has turned the bath's still waters a glorious blue.

'The *mikvah!*' cries the parish priest of *St Filippo Apostolo*, his words measured, metered out in acknowledgement of the sacredness of this place.

Our spirits leap in their various ways as we learn about the mikvah's perfection: even the three steps leading into the water have spiritual significance, the number 3 representing the spiritual harmony of opposites. And apparently it is not accidental that this holy bath is precisely 18 metres below street level.

'**18** is the symbol for "*chai*, the will of God",' says the lover of the mikvah, a simple, modern padre. It is our luck to have Father Phillip as our guide.

We gaze in absolute silence into waters that had been spiritually purified and nourished as memories of the Jewish faithful who once lived in Sicily.

Sadly, we are informed that those 14th-century Jews were asked to leave 'with one item of clothing and not much else besides' during one of Catholicism's darkest moments, the Inquisition.

'But they were invited to return one more time, in 1990. They didn't come, they didn't trust us,' says the present guardian of the Jewish treasure.

When we fall into a deep, respectful silence, I feel we are honouring the young Czech from Tel Aviv who is with us, and I suspect we are all thinking of the years of persecution, the Holocaust, and never, ever, ever forget.

<>

After some time, the young priest breaks from what has been a prayer cycle, and is suddenly nervous – though he appears eager to tell us something, which he soon does.

'Forgive me for informing you,' he says, deflecting to the four women, 'but it is not long ago that six Israeli soldiers asked to go down to the *mikvah*. It was amazing to have six Jews here. In the *mikvah*!' he cries, pausing and studying the waters, as though unsure to continue.

'And?' I ask, on all our behalf, keen to know the rest.

'But when they took all their clothes off,' he says with youthful embarrassment, 'the assistant priest and I didn't know where to look,' his face blushing in genuine innocence.

'Of course, I must remind you it is a long way down to the waters and Marco and I had waited at the top,' he says, by way of an uncalled-for apology.

There's a name etched on the wall above the *mikvah*. The priest sees us gazing at it.

Our new Jewish friend knows.

'This writing is ancient,' she says. 'The name is "Asher".'

A coy smile emerges, and we are told the word means 'happiness'.

Seeing we are caught up in it, Father Phillip breaks into our thoughts with great reverence.

'We think he is the man who made this *mikvah*,' says the keeper of Sicily's secret.

The young woman from Tel Aviv emerges from the closed-in world she has been in and nervously touches the young priest on the arm.

'Ah,' she says, and a tear drops upon her cheek, referencing the soldiers. 'I'm so pleased I came here, too.'

'But I wouldn't be game to take my clothes off,' she says, curiously biting her lips, and perhaps jealous that those cheeky young men had been able to purify.

'Thank you, Father Phillip,' she says in deep appreciation.

We know that it means so much to her to learn that the sacred purification bath is in safe hands. The young priest smiles and tells us he has the spring water that feeds his cherished *mikvah* quality-checked twice a year.

We had been there an hour and when we arrive back at the surface, we find nobody waiting. The great cathedral in the Piazza Duomo would be bustling with awestruck tourists. There'll be groups of schoolchildren among them who will be force-fed Christianity's stories, myths and legends, when all they need is the love that is being generated by the bonding of Jew and Christian in Sicily's sacred *mikvah* (the pact that, after centuries of conservative hatred, Pope John XXIII's Second Vatican Council had established when the pope absolved the Jews of any blame for Jesus' death).

Later, in 1965 to be precise, Pope Paul VI went on to condemn Catholic antisemitism finally to the past. It was a proclamation taken up by his successor, St John Paul II, who had also been at the Great Council; but it was the Polish Pope who did most to bring the words of reconciliation to action when he prayed at *Auschwitz* and established diplomatic ties with Israel.

Pope Francis continued to meet with Jewish leaders, while his meetings with the other great religions culminated in 2019 with a *pledge of human fraternity* made with the Grand Iman of Al-Alazar in Abu Dhabi, on February 4.

But for us, there's no less a brotherhood with Christ's family at this moment than the small Christian community we found in what had once been the Jewish neighbourhood of Syracuse, and the *mikvah* that has grounded the Christian Church of *St Filippo Apostolo*.

It is our good fortune to have met its chirpy parish priest wearing a simple T-shirt.

This young priest surely points the way of renewal of the Catholic Church; and we want to be part of the inspiration that sees his enthusiasm rewarded every day as he walks the old and new in the spirit of a loving God.

Phillip hopes we understand that he must leave us now because he must prepare for a meeting of the local *Comitato* – the committee he told us he had established to help run the tiny parish of *Chiesa di San Filippo Apostolo*, with its big story to tell.

We tell our new friend we have been fortunate to spend an hour with him.

'I am their poor servant,' he says, appreciative of our thanks, and we know that the *Chiesa de Filippo* is fortunate to have a priest of the new Church as leader of the parish – the excitable Father Phillip, a young man who is suddenly in a hurry not to disappoint his local community in old Syracuse.

We drop a few euros in the collection box and head out to dinner. Every Sicilian café with its house-made arancini balls and the famous *pasta sarde* that always looks different but always tastes the same.

I can't wait to tell others in the "community" church I belong to that we have a sister outside the institutional church in Sicily.

<><>

2017
Why I am a Catholic: Paul Coleman SJ

"It's my favourite because the Holy Spirit is the centrepiece of the artwork, and not subordinate to the Father and the Son."
FATHER JAMES MARTIN SJ, retired editor of the Jesuit online magazine *America*, reflecting on a stained-glass image of a dove in St Peter's Basilica.

<>

Paul Coleman SJ died on 25 September 2017; he was 93.

He could still pack a church, many of us loyalists, mentored by the priest we knew as "Paul" for most of our religious lives.

In my case, for some 42 years; ever since I had begun to call myself 'Catholic'.

I had called him 'the Jesuit' in deference to the Order of priesthood often described as there to keep the Catholic Church honest.

The Church hierarchy had tried to have the popular priest retire at 75 and again when he turned 85. But Paul was there for the long haul – and that meant until "death parted him" from his beloved believers of all manners and stripes.

Paul had had many run-ins with George Pell who desperately wanted him gone.

Father Paul Coleman was never one to boast, but he had remained proud to have thwarted the conservative group Opus Dei who, on more than one occasion had reported the popular priest to the hierarchy for the sin of "straying from the orthodox".

'What was I to do, George, when I was faced with a hundred worshippers seeking to be reconciled with God?' (And only one priest to perform face-to-face

"

reconciliation with each of them, in turn?)

How did the high-and-mighty cardinal react? 'You will call me "Eminence".'

<>

Paul Coleman's death saw the community he had left behind go on the search for like-minded priests and it was on his anniversary that one of those good men spoke as if he was still here.

'See, I can still draw a crowd,' I'm sure our friend Paul is saying.

'Paul was a priest for the people,' said Father Frank Brennan. 'With Paul, the ear always came before the voice.'

Brennan reminded us that our friend was also fiercely independent. '"We don't need to be putting up structures for dealing with social and political issues…it's all very well talking about these things, but what are people *doing?*" Paul Coleman would have said.'

<>

25th September 2017: Helen and I had arrived an hour before Paul's funeral service.

There was pandemonium in the streets; to the casual onlooker, someone important must have died, as police directed the traffic around the streets of North Sydney.

Where, in recognition of its city counterpart across the Harbour Bridge, the church here also bears the name St Mary's. While the Cathedral appears mighty, the real height lies in the North Sydney church, which dominates the northern skyline from its lofty perch on the highest hill.

Today, its capacity of 800 is already insufficient, and with fifteen minutes to go before kick-off, loudspeakers have been erected on the church grounds to accommodate the overflow.

St Mary's North Sydney had been the young Father Paul's first posting, and it was there, four decades earlier, that I had been given his extraordinary ear for human travails. In my time of questioning, with two children already, my chickens had finally come home, and, drug-free, I had begun to search out "The Way" – to God – the title of my first religious book, which had been gifted to me by the chaplain at the boarding school I had attended for five of the loneliest years of my life. I still own that book.

The chaplain was a good man. Reverend Sanders. He had once been both the school captain of Trinity Grammar and the First Fifteen rugby team. He could have mastered any walk of life, but Keith Sanders chose to enter the Church.

He had me doing the readings in our services and helping on the altar; that, perhaps, he saw as my training to follow the path he had taken himself.

Strange that it had fallen to a Catholic priest to quietly dispel my deep-seated concerns about – what I had come to see as – the 'mumbo jumbo of Jesus and Mary'.

It was Paul who convinced me to 'stop worrying about all that jazz of the resurrection, assumption and confession. Live a good life and love other people "as yourself".' (MARK: 12–30)

<>

There are *twenty-six* mostly aging clerics – perhaps all that's left locally from an ever-diminishing priesthood – clustered around the altar as the full Requiem Mass for Paul Coleman's funeral is about to begin.

We have been here for a while. Helen will be remembering the handsome priest with the chiselled features of a Romanesque head that most of her school, Loreto, had a crush on; while I am recalling the intellectual tussles I had had with Paul before I took the plunge.

So many good things were said at the "good-un's" funeral (Ian Lawther would have made him a mate). First, he was remembered as 'that fine priest who, even when he was dying himself, visited my husband in the Mater Hospital and gave him communion'.

'We don't just bury the remains of Paul Coleman here today. We bury something of ourselves. The most extraordinary thing about Paul was that he was absolutely inclusive,' said his close Jesuit friend, Michael Kelly.

'Paul's fame increased as he engaged with anyone, in need, or not,' said Jesuit leader Father David Strong, who has another name to add to his lifelong project, *The Dictionary of Jesuit Biography*: a page reserved for the name "Paul Coleman".

'I can hear him telling us to "just get on with life, get out there and do something, make a difference"', said Frank Brennan.

'When I last visited him in hospital, he said he was seeing life from the other side of the lake. The ever-independent Paul had fought the good fight to the end. He had run his race to the finish. He had kept the faith.'

'Like Rumi (the 13th-century Afghan poet Paul Coleman also admired), our friend Paul is saying to us now: "I can't really explain what it's like where I live. But someday I will meet you there."'

'Paul Coleman gambled everything for love,' concluded Brennan, the human rights lawyer and social justice advocate.

And so it went on. The last words were given to poet and cartoonist, the pixie-like Michael Leunig:

'We've made it through. We will survive.
The soil is sweet, and love is still alive.
The bell of happiness is ringing.
A little bird inside our heart is singing.'

<>

Two days before Paul Coleman SJ died, Helen and I visited our friend who had mentored us both; my wife from her school days, her uber-questioning husband upon my return from the UK in 1968.

On that day, I had returned yet another book Paul had been eager for me to read: *The Cosmic Christ** – Jesus there at the Creation, Jesus in nature and all around us, now and forever. (*Hans-Werner Shroeder, 2010)

The book had arrived in my hands with numerous yellow Post-it strips at irregular intervals between its 256 pages; "read this", they proclaimed.

The book states: "love" is mentioned on 541 occasions in the Bible, "love one another" 59 times.

Paul Coleman had summed it all up with a quote from Jeremiah (31–33) that defines the personal priestly ministry he had left behind: "The law is written on your heart."

Therein lies the last will and testament of Father Paul Vincent Coleman SJ.

And now Paul's legacy lives on in a small church overlooking Sydney Harbour. It is where, after flatly refusing retirement, our friend had established an ever-growing community off the institutional grid in which "doing something for others" is never a byword.

We can still remember the day our dying friend went AWOL from the hospital and ministered to us at Sunday Mass for the last time. Later that Sunday, Paul slipped into the coma that was to claim him three days later.

He left behind a vibrant congregation, one that is envied to this day.

Vale, Paul Coleman SJ.

Here's Rumi again:

"Lovers of God,
sometimes a door opens,
and a human being becomes a way
for grace to come through."

<>

"Paul's church" – our church - stands conspicuously on the rolling hills to the south of Sydney Harbour. Managed by us, the "people of God", we invite certain priests of our choosing to minister to us; by so doing, we avoid the politics of the institutional Church.

While we don't "tithe", we seek out good things to do, and a recent charitable drive saw us help a Ugandan couple who had fled a country that had wanted to murder them; forced to leave their five children behind in Catholic care, by the time those kids arrived, their parents were already Australian citizens. We had helped the family be united, as "Aussies", one and all.

I recently asked a fellow traveller what keeps her coming back to our non-institutional Church?

'Grace,' she said.

Did she mean 'kindness and compassion' by that? Or, perhaps Pope Francis' favourite word, 'mercy'?

'Grace,' she replied. It encompasses everything.

"To find a religion, find a community," says outspoken nun Sister Joan Chittister. A rabid advocate for equality, justice and peace, a recent biography describes the feisty female as "Saint" Joan. *(From Certainty to Faith*, Tom Roberts, 2015)

<><>

2023
Why I am a Catholic: 1. Belief

He was at Mass on a recent Sunday morning when, studying the large print of an icon depicting the resurrection, he was thrown into a 'swoon' – he said, 'when an angel suddenly appeared'.

Tiny, the spirit 'was in the top right corner of the old painting,' he said specifically.

Describing it as a 'small luminous winged creature with piercing eyes,' he says he saw the apparition raise a long, slender finger.

'And it – male or female I wasn't sure, it was such an androgynous figure – it was *beckoning* me. "Come closer," a voice in my head was saying.'

When my friend went to stand, he says he found he was glued to his seat, and neither could he take his eyes off the icon. Apparently, he maintained that posture through to the end of the service.

He said it was only then that the angel slowly faded away, along with the final notes of the recessional hymn.

Which was?

'*Strong and Constant – is my love.* For me, for us, for us believers.' he said.

<>

I have known Frederick for over 30 years and am used to his stories; it was Fred, after all, who had once climbed the steps to the shrine in Medjugorje – on his knees!

And, what's more, it was in a time of war. The war of Bosnia/Herzegovina. He told me he had met an old woman who said she was one of the two small girls who had claimed to have seen a vision of the Virgin Mary.

The experience had Fred chasing sightings of Mary all over the world: Lourdes, Fatima, Guadeloupe.

Fred is the most singularly superstitious "believer" I have ever known. He once had a sage in tow who would give him envelopes, not to be opened until a certain date, when it would often turn out to be investment advice: he was once told to "buy gold".

Fred's believing nature can be on the unnerving side of sanity, but it can also be truly beautiful.

He is a man of charity. He can be generous to a fault with his seemingly untold wealth.

Wherever Fred is in the world, he is like the American Express card itself, he never "leaves home without it".

I've seen him stuff a pile of banknotes of the local currency in his pocket; money for any beggars he comes across, he dishes them out readily, unable to pass by someone down on their luck.

Fred is South African and there's a story told that he was once on the road heading into Johannesburg when he came across a black man holding up a large sign that read: "PLEASE HELP IN JESUS' NAME."

Stopping instantly, he approached the man, who said in greeting: 'Good morning, sah.' The beggar wore an apprehensive look, expecting charity.

Of course, Fred would oblige, but his first words were a surprise to the poor man: 'I would like to buy your sign,' said Fred.

'Oh, I'm sorry to tell you, sah – this sign is not for sale,' said the beggar.

When he proceeded to clutch the sign tightly to his chest, Fred became even more determined.

'I'll give you fifty rand.'

'No.'

Fred upped the offer; said he'd pay a hundred rand.

'Two hundred rand?'

'No. You can't have my sign,' said the beggar. 'This sign is not for sale.'

'Why on Earth – why?'

'God gave me this sign,' said the beggar.

Fred gave him all the money he had on him, and to this day he will tell you he met Jesus that day 'on the road to Emmaus'.

Not far from Johannesburg.

<>

Fred's stories are instructive of my belief that we all need something to keep us together, in our skin, as human beings.

Whatever that is – how crazy others may think it is – it's not mine to argue with.

"Faith, – it is said these days, "cannot be taught, it can only be caught".

I married a woman of faith.

But it is not that simple. Helen is a questioner, a realist sceptical of much she is told.

My Emmaus Road began with my wife.

But that was before I discovered Arnold Toynbee's "twin pillars of religion", and I spent the years 1975-76 badgering a Christ-like Jesuit, and a man known as "Australia's Last Communist". (Arnold Toynbee's 6-volume *Study of History* describes the 20th century as "the battle for hearts and minds between Christianity and Communism".)

Father Paul Coleman was instructive in telling me that following Jesus is simply about striving to be a 'good person, living for others, with compassion and love'.

"The greater of these is *LOVE*." (1 Corinthians:13)

While a deeply spiritual believer, Paul Coleman was never heard to pontificate, ever, about anything. Paul had spent a lifetime listening.

'We cannot know it all,' he said, giving me that book in the weeks before his death. *The Cosmic Christ* could be another gospel. I miss my friend, Paul.

<>

Author, Frank Hardy, whose best-known novel was *Power Without Glory*, died in 1994. He was 77; a writer in the realist school that includes Dickens and Balzac. Today's reader would also do well to read Hardy's criticism of how our country has treated its original inhabitants, *The Unlucky Australians*.

Hardy wasn't an easy man. He reminded me of John Osborne, an early champion of the English working poor, his best-known novel, *Look Back in Anger*. I wrote to Phillip Adams once about my "year with Hardy", and the ABC radio presenter wrote back saying: "Frank Hardy was a Stalinist and a con man until the day he died."

He was all that, and more: egotistical, "agin" the government; but I remember he had respect for the Jesuits and especially one of the Order's priests – Father Paul Coleman.

We often lunched together, the three of us; Paul didn't budge when Hardy expressed the idea that Jesus was 'the first communist'.

Ironically, it was the communist Hardy who played the final role in the trifecta of influencers of my journey to faith.

<>

The 1930's Depression had seen Frank Hardy's father, Thomas, join the "International Workers of the World".

Tom was often at meetings; his son usually being towed along.

Winifred Hardy had named her first-born "Francis", after the poor man of Assisi and, a staunch Catholic, her "meetings" with Saint Francis were a ritual attendance at Mass every day.

Socialism vs Catholicism was the constant agenda in the Hardy household.

Consequently, it was a lively household, and the young Frank would hear his parents arguing into the night.

While the language got to be violent, it was never physical and ended with Tom Hardy throwing tea towels over the religious statues.

He would turn around the icons that covered the Hardy's walls.

How did it all end?

Frank told me: 'Next morning, Winnie would get up in the dark and put everything back where it was.'

Ship righted, until the next time.

The upshot?

'Nothing was ever said.'

The Frank Hardy I knew was ever proud of his mum.

But I have never seen a man defer to another as Frank did to my Jesuit friend.

Nevertheless, when it is all said and done, Hardy was a gambler and the last time I saw him, he asked me to place five each way on a horse for him.

'Do the numbers,' he said, echoing astrology. The horse is carrying number 7 saddle cloth, it's in barrier 7 and (you can guess) it's running in race 7.'

'It's also the only horse in the race that's won at the track, and distance, mate,' he had added for good measure. 'Can't lose,' said Hardy.

Came seventh, and I am still waiting for the tenner.

<>

So: Helen, Frank and Paul, and it was all three in my soul that day in late summer, 1976 when we were holidaying in the big river country of northern NSW. I had asked my wife to 'please stop for a moment at that public phone booth' on the way back to our digs.

'Who did I have to speak with? So suddenly?' I was asked, upon returning to the car.

'Father Paul.'

'Why?'

'I have just become a Catholic.'

'Oh,' Helen said, totally unsurprised.

My wife knows me better than I do myself; what's news about that?

<>

And what sort of Catholic am I? Are we?

I am reminded of the great American philosopher and intellectual H.L. Mencken, who said:

"While morality is doing what you believe to be right, no matter what you are told, religion is doing what you are told, no matter what is right."

So: that's one down against the idea of *Institution* that I see as controlling and lacking empathy.

As for "the meaning of life", Alice B. Toklas asked her life partner, writer Gertrude Stein, once – after her years of studying the human condition: "What is the answer?"

"No, my dear," said Stein.

"What is the question?" (The Autobiography of Alice B. Toklas by Gertrude Stein).

<><>

2023
Why I am a Catholic: 2. Faith

Here's a very short story, Father Paul Coleman – "The Jesuit" - told me once:

There's a monastery in the mountains far away, where all had been well, very well with the monks. Until…

Until it wasn't: after all the years living in harmony the glue that had held them together went missing.

The community had lost its faith.

'What's so wonderful now?'

Brother Thomas, the youngest, wants to ask of the old Abbot, his doubt sorely tested.

'Where's the meaning of life…where's the purpose, now?' his inner voice is shouting.

'You're the one with all the ideas,' he wants to say to the Abbot. 'Do something.'

The Abbot was unperturbed. The young are always questioning and doubting. He turned his kind eyes upon Thomas. Softly spoken, the Abbot said to him: 'We must hear from the wise man. You are the fittest among us, my son. You must go to the wise man at once. We will remain here and pray.'

'Prayer? Isn't that what has left us?' one of the old monks said under his breath.

So Thomas set out across the waters and into the valleys and, after a climb that would have been too much for the other monks, he found the wise man seemingly waiting for his young visitor.

He was given a drink of the purest water and some nuts and insects (glad to have been well fed by sympathetic villagers along the way!) and, pouring out the monastery's grief, he explained his mission while the wise man nodded continually. It was as though he had always been in the know.

Finally, the wise man placed his old, gnarled hand on that of his visitor and gazed at young Thomas with compassionate, revealing eyes.

'Go,' he said. 'Go and tell your Abbot this: "Christ is among you."'

So Thomas the doubter took off, and at a much faster pace than before, in great agitation and carrying this mystery with him.

'What did he say?' inquired the first of his fellow monks, who he came across in the monastery garden leaning languidly on a shovel that had lain idle for weeks.

The other monks soon gathered about their young messenger and, hoping him to be the bearer of good news, they followed him through the cloisters and into the Abbot's room.

'Well?' asked the Abbot expectantly of young Thomas, who had fallen into a sudden anxiety. After all, he had been repeating the words the Abbot had given him over and over in his mind, hoping he had got them right.

'Well? Don't be nervous,' said the Abbot, as all the monks began displaying their desperation in mutterings and physical unease. 'What did he say?' asked the Abbot, who was the only one among them who knew their collective patience was surely about to be rewarded.

Thomas began his short dissertation with a bout of stuttering, but he soon pulled himself together, and the answer the monastery had long waiting for fell out of his mouth like a biblical pronouncement:

'He said that one of us is Jesus,' the youngest of the monks replied, looking from one to the other of his friends, who were all gathered there.

There was an immediate, eager bustling among them, as words of recognition dawned upon them suddenly from the Abbot to the lowliest among them.

What if? (Such is my belief: "We are Body, Mind – and **Spirit**. *The Love of Jesus Within*.)

<><>

2025
The Pope is Dead, Long Live the Pope

Monday April 26. It is five days since Pope Francis died and the red-hatted, red-clothed cardinals in solemn procession drifting across St Peter's Square, are in stark contrast to their leader who in, eschewing the medieval, chose a simple peasant habit.

Francis will also be buried in the black workman's shoes he had favoured from the beginning of his 12-year papacy.

Neither will his tomb reside among the popes of yesteryear in *St Peter's*; no, Pope Francis had chosen a simple niche in a wall of the basilica, *Santa Maria Maggiore*, outside Vatican City where the Pope would often pray among the people.

There, a single white rose was placed and, above it the name he had been known by:

FRANCISCUS.

The Pope is dead. Long live the Pope.

Father Mick's "Frankie" lives on - in us.

The "people of God". Forever more.

Eighty per cent of the current 253 cardinals owe their places to Pope Francis and only 135, being under the required voting age of 80, will attend the secretive conclave that will elect the new pope from among them.

Francis had made it through Easter, having to watch others wash the feet of prisoners – he, having performed the sacred ritual every year of his pontificate.

He had determined to follow in the footsteps of the great reformist Pope, John XX111, and I wonder now, gazing at this solemn sea of red: *"Where were you, cardinals, when Frankie needed your help?"*

<><><>

AFTERWORD
Forging on for Justice

Chrissie Foster remains in the eye of the storm.

We first met on a bleak autumn day in 2023.

Away from the cameras, her anger contained, this remarkable survivor appears calmer; a beautiful woman, her greying hair swept in curls about her perfectly proportioned face, she could be a film star. I am taken by eyes, the stories they tell, and Chrissie's in the flesh are curiously engaging and at once revealing of the determination that has preceded her; I suspect it is not entirely my imagination that has me seeing in their depths a raging strength, easily comprehended.

Strength borne out of suffering.

Chrissie had been pleased to see the previous night's *60 Minutes* emerge with the video footage of George Pell's outrageous admission that he had lied when he said he had never seen the self-harming photo of Emma Foster. Chrissie says *Channel 9* showed the incriminating footage 'as a tribute to (her late husband) Anthony'.

While unsurprising to those "in the know", such a public airing is a reminder of Pell's total lack of empathy and the cardinal's determination to protect himself at all costs.

George Pell sought power over his fellow man, right from the start.

The man, who presumably thought he was some kind of super being – deserving perhaps of being pope? – has "left the building now".

But Chrissie Foster remains, and this book joins the bravest of the brave in continuing the fight for truth and justice. Not so powerful now, that once powerful male-dominated institution that is the Catholic Church.

"God and I are not speaking," Chrissie says at the end of her book, *Still Standing*.

Although sometimes in my darkest moments", she writes, "I have said a little prayer."

She says her experience had been to act instead of praying for help.

"This is not what the priesthood hoped for. They wanted paralysed people on their knees who prayed – not acted – while they *preyed*," she says.

"NEVER FORGET," say the Jews.

It must be said also of that vast litany of victims of priests and others: never forget the children.

Compelled as I was from the start ("I need your help" – in covering up those crimes) the unchanging focus of this book has always been about them.

Shame on all those who dare to suggest those rapes and suicides be consigned to the dustbin of history.

Shame on those who say we should put them behind us.

We are not "dwelling on old wounds", as Archbishop Fisher said. We are talking about the Church's failure to protect children.

The "Little Ones" Pope Francis acknowledged on the first day of his remarkable papacy. He also said: he is simply one of us.

The People of God.

Eight
APPENDICES

APPENDIX
Ian Lawther's Letter to Pope Benedict

Dear Pope Benedict,

I heard the other day that you apologised to five people in America who have been abused by Roman Catholic priests.

Unfortunately, I feel that, like all the Catholic Church's efforts to deal with clergy sexual abuse, this was a gesture designed to protect the good name of the Church.

But you were not the one who had to lay awake at night, wondering if the car travelling at breakneck speed, disappearing in the distance, was the last time you would hear your son, a victim of a now convicted Roman Catholic priest, alive.

You were not the one who had to take your son to hospital at 2.30 in the morning, because he had broken three bones in his hand, in a fit of anger and guilt, because his mind had been so poisoned, that the priest was able to convince him everything was his fault.

You were not the one who had to work harder than any man should have to work, to keep a fractured family together. And you were not the one that was forced to watch your son's belief in God smashed beyond repair. This and much, much more happened to me.

It has caused me to go completely blind in the left eye, following the realisation that the same priest, who molested my son, baptised my seven-day old daughter a couple of months after he first molested my son.

All this was capped off by the priest I reported it to, saying to my wife and I, 'Oh yes, this man has a reputation for this sort of thing'. I can't possibly express the anger I feel when I think about this, knowing that this priest and other people in the hierarchy of the organisation you head, knew of this man's reputation as an abuser of children, yet chose to let him loose among our children.

I was forced to agree to bring my children up as Catholic so my wife could marry in the Church of her faith. I took this promise seriously, only to find that the Catholic Church feels it has absolutely no duty of care or sense of protection towards my children.

The Church has shown a blatant disregard for my son's welfare, and the welfare of my family, so the family I envisaged that I would have as an old man, is vastly different from the reality I now face. The sexual and psychological abuse by the priest and the disregard from the Church shown towards my family, especially to my son, means that he will never know what comfort could be possible to obtain from the Church.

I know of people who have lost young family members, who could not face the world with the guilt instilled in them by the priests who raped, sodomised, and abused them.

I know teachers who have lost jobs, because they felt it was their duty to report priests, when children in their care reported to them that they did not like the way priests touched them.

With one fraction of the effort you put into a press release, you could pick up a pen and make it possible for priests to marry; you could announce a zero-tolerance policy for child molesters; you could prevent paedophile men from signing up to train for the priesthood.

How can it be that your organisation can train a priest for seven years and not pick up any psychological problems in that time, but teachers with minimum training in paedophile behaviour, can recognise enough grooming signs to sound their warning bells, after a few weeks? However, if they do what any parent would expect them to do, they will be forced out of their jobs, their careers, with their futures in tatters in every possible way.

My son was sexually and psychologically abused by a parish priest, of your Melbourne Church, for over three years. My son lived with the guilt for another three years, and then was further abused for another five years, by the system that the Catholic Church has in place in Melbourne.

The use of time as a weapon; keeping victims waiting for months and months, even years; is just another form of abuse, but this time organised by the Melbourne Church Response.

The efforts of the Melbourne Response professionals to minimise abuse can only be regarded by victims as collusive self-preservation by the Melbourne Archdiocese operating like some large corporations. The Melbourne system needs thorough evaluation and overhaul by truly independent professionals.

Dear Pope, if you are genuinely sorry about the lives of victims, their families, parishioners, and others affected by clergy abuse, I ask that you do something constructive.

1.   Don't allow any more false promises, and let parents know who does accept responsibility for the welfare and protection of their children.

2.   If you're fair dinkum about Human Rights, let your espoused concern be directed to the hurting masses of people, whose lives have been decimated by this great hidden scourge of the Church's sexual abuse scandal, and allow the true figures of the numbers of clergy sexual abusers to be published.

3.   If you're fair dinkum, provide funding for education of hierarchy, clergy, teachers through the school systems, for parents and children in parishes. Use programs from the community, already developed by secular professionals. This would take up a fraction of the energy and finances the Catholic Church is investing in World Youth Day.

4.   If you're fair dinkum, fund true listening and healing programs for the sexually abused, their families and people in the parishes. This would take seriously the need for restoration and reconciliation across all these important and neglected people.

5.   If you're fair dinkum about providing healing and hope for us all, and you have no ulterior motive to attract young people back to the Church, introduce a broad-spectrum policy of absolute truth from the absolute beginning.

Pope Benedict, you can be the first pope in history to recognise the historical enormity of the wounds of clergy sexual abuse and to move the Church forward to act to heal these wounds.

For the last five years your bishops refused to meet with us, leaving us with absolutely no option but to communicate with you by these public means. Will you meet with us, or instruct your bishops to match their actions to your recent promises?

There are already over one hundred Australian priests convicted of sexual abuse and many more have been dealt with secretly by the Church...BEFORE ANOTHER CHILD IS ABUSED, PLEASE ACT!

Yours sincerely,

Ian Lawther

24th April 2004

<><><>

ACKNOWLEDGEMENTS

Grateful thanks and appreciation to my wife for her belief in this book and constant support. Helen is my best friend and had cast her critical eye over all my attempts at writing a story that blindsided us both at first, but we knew had to be told. Nothing cuts deeper into the heart – for a child especially! - than to be betrayed, and that *Betrayal* was the focus that kept the book's momentum alive.

Much appreciation to our friend Eva Setton who has also been seemingly happy to endure reading every manuscript I placed in front of her over all the years. "Writers write", there is no alternative, Virginia Woolf once said.

I am eternally grateful to Cathy Wilcox, for the use of her illustration for the front cover. Cathy has a talent that cuts to the chase and truly reflects the notion that every picture tells a story. The award-winning illustrator's daily masterpieces are a major reason to buy the Sydney Morning Herald, and Melbourne Age newspapers.

Thanks to all those who helped me immeasurably by reading the various manuscripts and were generous with their suggestions.

Tim Ayliffe's editorial instinct was invaluable in keeping *Betrayal* on its path, as my personal story. I had the help and support of all my loving family: our other boys, Matthew, Ben, and Sam; my brother David; and our sister Janet Flarey.

Thanks to Gail Gill and Michelle Smith; two brave women whose special insights, gained from long years employed at executive levels in Catholic Education and Administration were absolute gifts to the story; their work in various communities provided a backdrop of relevance that has greatly helped.

I deeply acknowledge the help freely given to me by Doctor Robert Gordon MBBS DPM FRANZCP. Bob is an eminent psychiatrist and the important contribution he and his colleagues made towards my understanding of paedophilia was of great help; the important work they do has aided in strengthening Australian laws. My thanks to the NSW Child Protection Council.

Newly formed some 40 years ago, time has not dimmed those deep conversations I had with the courageous woman who appears in *Betrayal* as "Gemma".

I acknowledge the Hon Julia Gillard AC, who, as well as being Australia's first woman Prime Minister, will also go down in Australian political history as having created the Royal Commission into Institutional Responses to Child Sexual Abuse.

My many talks with Chrissie Foster and Ian Lawther remain foremost in revealing the true horrors they and their families endured at the hands of priests and clerics.

I am indebted to the many conversations I had with the amazing Dee McBride, who endured terrible experiences with priests who thought that country NSW shielded them from being found out. Dee endured numerous battles with the police, and her bravery in talking to me is to be admired. Her story is a striking indictment of a church on its knees. I keep meeting people with stories of horror and deceit, and I appreciated their willingness to share their truths with me.

Broken Rites has made a massive compendium of church crimes against children, and I am deeply thankful for all I learnt there. *brokenrites.org.au.*

I acknowledge all those who have travelled alongside me over the long years of writing *Betrayal*. 'There is no such thing as good writing, there's only good rewriting," Truman Capote once said; that is a tall order, and although my intermittent doubts and general laziness often got in the way, and I hoped I wasn't climbing a mountain that never ends Capote's words compelled me to forge on with the ardour of the many drafts I wrote.

Others who always had my back include Pam Sprouster, Terry Carr, Tony Stubley, Beverley Roche, Therese Wildschut, Jill Gavin, Louise Smith, Jim "Nick" Nichol, Fordie, Anne Moss, Joan Geyle, Trish Austin, Bernie Deverson (and other life-travellers of Helen and mine known as "The Daggs").

Some early supporters are deceased, and they include my first publisher, Alan Halbish, retired Justice of the Family Court Bryce Ross-Jones, and one-time Senator Colin "Jim" Mason. I received welcome advice from author friends who have passed, including Derek Hansen. Bryce Courtenay, in his inimitable way, urged me on, and more recently, Bryce's son, and writer of history novels,

Adam Courtenay. Others who offered good advice remain anonymous.

Finally, thanks to my literary agent, Jeanne Rycksman of Key People Literary Management. Jeanne's skill at identifying the "right" publisher has brought *Betrayal* to Fair Play Publishing and its principal, Bonita Mersiades.

I am indebted to all the talented people at Fair Play for the book's production; their dedication is admirable. John Coomer proved to be a first-rate editor, and John and Bonita picked up from where I left off. Others who contributed to *Betrayal's* production include designer Leslie Priestley and the PR team appointed by Fair Play, led by Debbie McInnes.

My Reading

Early advice from an author relative, the poet Ruth Bedford, that one should read everything out there on your subject proved critical.

Top of the pile are *Hell on the Way to Heaven* and *Still Standing* by Chrissie Foster and Paul Kennedy.

The Priests by David Miller is an account of being abused by two priests as a child.

Louise Milligan's *Cardinal: The Rise and Fall of George Pell* and *Witness,* published by Milligan after Pell's Trial.

A Guest at the Feast, by Irish writer Colm Toibin, shortlisted three-times for the Booker Prize.

The Sins of the Father, by Australian literary giant, Thomas Keneally.

Father Michael Kelly SJ's essay entitled *Shirtfronting*.

I kept returning to *Lolita* by Vladimir Nabakov for the author's masterly exploration of the nature of a paedophile.

Wounded Shepherd by Austen Ivereigh is my favourite biography of Pope Francis.

And so it goes.

ABOUT THE AUTHOR

J S Ayliffe is a Sydney-based author.

Like many before him, John cut his teeth in advertising, working in both Sydney and London.

He lives with his wife of almost 60 years, Helen, on Sydney's Northern Beaches. They have four sons: the crime fiction writer, Tim, composer and musician, Matthew, Sam is a "finance whizz", while Ben has staked his claim in advertising,

Betrayal is John's fifth book.

Previous books (published as John Stephen Ayliffe):

Blind Man's Bluff.
The Priest's Woman and Other Stories.
My Brother's Eyes by David and John Ayliffe
Icons

More really good books from Fair Play Publishing

Jumping Jack

Home, Forever

A Secret Grief

The Coping Stone

Turning The Tide

Socceroos in Scotland

Big Con

Football Fans
In Their Own Write...

Available from
fairplaypublishing.com.au/shop
and all good bookstores